ARISING BY ONESELF

*The Artistic Way of
Climbing Towards Success*

ADVENT AM MONYATSIWA

 www.trafford.com

North America & international
toll-free: 1 888 232 4444 (USA & Canada)
fax: 812 355 4082

Contents

DEDICATION

I dedicate this book to the total well being of my mother Africa; particularly to my country, Botswana and to all the Third World or Developing Countries around the world, where the wisdom of the things I write about is scarce. It is substantially dedicated to all individuals who are struggling to deal with themselves and are tormented by the fact that no matter how hard they try, they always find themselves to be doing the very same thing that they try hard not to do.

ACKNOWLEDGEMENT

I am deeply indebted to my respectable nation of Botswana, hoping to add to its solemn rule of democracy and its freedom from civil wars; to my beloved and admired mother, whom without her persistent love, guidance, support and encouragement I would have given up on life and my dreams many times over. To Best Kaisara for helping me in doing the necessary research on animals and to Otsile Chris Kootsene for standing side by side with me in my pursuit to publish my books. The inspiration to write and publish this excerpt from "ARISINGS" came from my personal rising and falling in my past negative and positive circumstances, especially those of dealing with my inner self when nobody is around. However, it is through relating with relatives and friends around the world; acquaintances, past situations and things; places and countries like America, Algeria and Japan that I learn to effectively deal with and arise by myself. Hence I must acknowledge and give gratitude to ALL. My greatest acknowledgement and gratitude, however, goes to God; *It is through learning and studying the ways of God that I learn to deal, relate and arise by myself effectively.*

PREFACE

*A*rising By Oneself is yet another book excerpt under the total book *ARISINGS*, which is also a series under *The Art of Life*. *ARISINGS* talks about four ways in which a person can arise himself from any undesired circumstance to any favorable position he or she may wish in life. These four ways are:

1. *Arising By Falling*
2. *Arising By People*
3. *Arising By Oneself*, and
4. *Arising By God;*

In this book however, we focus on the several ways, methods or techniques in which one can arise by oneself. That is how one can independently arise by one's own effort, under one's own steam and on one's own initiative, especially through the personal-initiative to make decisions and take steps which most ordinary people are either afraid or simply neglect to take.

INTRODUCTION

In the book *Arisings*, we talked about *Arising by Falling* which showed us how to use problems, adversities and hardships as a ladder in which we can arise ourselves higher into a life of success and contentment. The personal self-talk philosophy you can take from it is this:

Your Down Moments are your best Possibilities for Growth, Your greatest Pains are a way to develop your greatest Resistance, Your worst Failures indeed highlight your Success, Your Loses, your best motivation to Achieve. Your Suffering, your best time for gaining true Wisdom, Your worst Struggles in life indeed are a door way to Greatness, Your closed Doors are but an opportunity to seek fresh Ideas, Your troubles, create your Legacy.

Your Loneliness, your teacher of Self-Reliance,
Your Risks, your opportunities to reinforce personal Initiative,
Your Criticisms, your way to learning more about Yourself,
Your enemies, your inspiration to act in Love.

Your Fears are the keys that unlock your Courage,
Your Solitude, indeed your time to seek peace and Enlightenment,
Your Hunger, a chance to realize the impermanence of the Body,
And your Death, a time for your soul to experience Freedom!
You see, It is by getting burnt that You learn
not to mess around with fire.
It is by getting punched in the face that
You learn to protect yourself,
It is by getting things wrong that You learn the right way to do things,

> *It is by lowering your body first that you*
> *can lift yourself off the ground.*

> *It is by climbing up the hill that You develop*
> *the strongest forward motion,*
> *It is by taking a step back that You can see*
> *clearly that which is too close to perceive,*
> *It is by pushing the biggest rocks in life that You*
> *develop the strongest will and character.*
> *It is clear then that to advance to higher altitudes*
> *in life We must first experience the low falls.*

> *The ground is the base in which we can push ourselves*
> *off to the moon, without it no flight is possible!*
> *You See, We Arise By Falling!*

Then in the book *Arising by People*, we discussed a great deal about the art of dealing with people, because in order to arise higher than your paper qualifications can take you, you must be able to deal with people successfully. Yet one can understand and see through others better only when he can understand and see through himself. Therefore to deal with others effectively requires one to be able to deal with himself masterfully. This is where *Arising By Oneself* comes in; to help you learn the greatest art of them all—Self-Mastery—The inner ability to be able to understand, manage and handle yourself in a manner that is pleasing to yourself and your environment.

The result of which you will begin to see life as a canvas in which to paint your desired destiny using all the skills you already possess including that of dealing with people. You will learn how to control the external and internal influences that affect you daily decision. You will learn how to solve the problems and adversities that life may throw at you by using the mathematical formulas of life, given by life itself. You will learn the art of arising by managing the self, which having mastered, arising by other people and by your environment will be like taking a walk in park. Moreover, you will understand the fundamental and unchanging laws of success that bring about material riches, prosperity and greatness. So that, whatever it is that you will purpose in your heart to get, and by creating sound plans backed up by resolute actions marked by unwavering faith, you will no doubt get it.

Now I will not get into the details of how to accumulate such material riches, as my principal focus in this book is to share with you the art in which you can arise yourself within unfavorable life circumstance to favorable paths that can lead you to your desired life of success, contentment and of course ultimately the riches you want.

That said, I shall briefly only touch on the following topics so that you can utilize them as the vehicles in which you can ride and arise to your desired destination. In other words, they shall be the weapons which you will employ in your defense against the adversities and arrows of life:

1. The Art of Self-Management,
2. The Artistic Life,
3. The Art of Success,
4. The Mathematics of Life,
5. The Art of Financial Freedom

ARISING BY THE
SELF-MANAGEMENT SYSTEM

The art of managing the self leads to the art of knowing oneself. In this particular topic, I will describe to you a system which I developed for myself in order to manage and keep myself under control, because, in the end, *self-control is the best form of self-management.*

Keep in mind that the art of self-management is not limited to the following system alone; the system is shaped according to the way I live my life. You are encouraged to create your own system of self-management that is in accordance with your own personal-lifestyle. Use the system that is described below only as an eye-opener and a guide to creating your own unique self-management system:

1. Genuine Self-Love
2. Positive Self-Counsel
3. Positive Self-Talk
4. Detachment
5. Meditation

1. Genuine Self-Love:

(The counteraction to doing the things that cause harm to your total wellbeing; be it physical, spiritual, mental, emotional, social or financial)

First of all, by self-love I am not referring to narcissism or any type of egotism, hence I say genuine self-love. Self-Management begins first by loving your "self" because by loving yourself you will abandon the things that cause suffering into your life and forsake the thoughts, emotions and actions that cause you to do the things that harm your body, mind and spirit For example, if one loves himself, he will love his body and thus to get addicted to drugs; alcohol, cocaine, etcetera, would be a detestable thing and he will do all that he can to avoid them and if he is already in the middle of the addiction, he will always be open to change and continue to find ways in which he can come out from them.

In other words, just like you will do a lot to protect your loved ones from any imminent danger including themselves, you will also do the same and more to protect yourself because you love yourself. Also by loving yourself, you will be mindful and open to ideas that can do you some good irrespective of where or whom they come from. You see, whether the ideas are from yourself, friends, family, enemies or lunatics; you will look beyond what they appear to be and see that which is hidden within them that can benefit you in some way. In simple, a person who loves himself will do anything to learn about himself and how to take care of his needs, desires and wants.

For instance, have you noticed how some people are obsessed with cars? How they will do anything to keep it clean and free from scratches? Now, of course, this is a bit too much because it is getting overly attached to material things that do not last, but imagine if people loved themselves like this? Would they take in narcotics and or eat foods that harm their mind, body and total well-being?

Again, I am not suggesting that people become narcissistic and egomaniacal here, because narcissism and egomania are no difference from hating and torturing yourself. The results are ultimately the same because they destroy you! One must learn to balance things and thus balance his life. Look, it is not that some people do not love themselves, every person ultimately loves himself no matter what they do and not do. It is just that some people are unmindful of their well-being and oblivious of what is happening to them either through their environment or their own actions.

Also, it is not that they do not care about themselves either, they simple do not think about themselves lovingly. That is they do not think about their body, their mind, their emotions and their souls because a majority of their time is spent in obsessing about the things that are external to themselves. They are excessively attached to these external things and so they do not see the damage they could be doing to themselves inwardly and outwardly. For example, in the anorexic person's delusional worry of what other people are thinking about his or her looks, he or she indirectly damages the mind and body through his or her obsessive attempts to lose weight.

Genuine self-love requires that you are mindful of these things, that you know exactly what harms you and how to avoid or get rid of it. Therefore when you genuinely love yourself, you will naturally identify your own uniqueness in terms of your weaknesses and strengths in physical talents, appearances, mental and emotional capacities. Then once you know and are aware of these things about yourself, you plan what to do about them; how to capitalize on your strengths and strengthen your weaknesses. But to strengthen yourself does not mean that you must overly criticize yourself or excessively judge yourself; your appearances, your mistakes, your failures and past experiences.

You ought not to expect too much from yourself. Instead, you must love yourself without any expectations and attachments so that you are not moved negatively by what you discover about yourself. You must accept yourself without the feelings of judgment but the natural desire to improve who you are. Only then will you not harm yourself nor take for granted the beautiful being that you already are. You see, it is only *by accepting yourself completely, with understanding and without any partiality that you can then love yourself freely and sincerely as you are*.

Just simply telling yourself that you love yourself is not enough. You must take actions that show your deep-rooted inner-self that you indeed love yourself. For example, you can reward yourself on every little or big accomplishment you make. If nobody throws a birthday party for you, throw one for yourself, if you get promoted in your career, throw a small celebration for yourself as a sign of respect and acknowledgement of yourself. In other words, do not wait for other people to congratulate you or tell you good things about yourself, YOU yourself must be pleased and content within yourself and by yourself regardless of what other people say or not say. *You do not let external influences to influence who you are*. In the end loving yourself is something that you must initiate and experience by yourself for only you know what makes you; what makes you feel loved and what does not.

In conclusion, if you love yourself, keeping a healthy-being by developing healthy practices would be a natural habit to you. This is because *you will love the health of your body more than you love the drug that deteriorates it*. You will love the positive mental attitude and the positive dealings with others more than you love the criticisms, complains and blames that not only destroy your clear judgment but also your potential to make friends. You will love the feelings of love, happiness and peace more than you love to indulge in the feelings of anger, hatred and sadism that bring about distress in your life. You will love building people up more than you love to hear and talk about the rumors that destroy your relationship with them.

You see now, you must love your health more than you love that which feels good but ultimately causes harm to your well-being—You must love your plans and goals more than you love those things that entertain you but keep you away from achieving them. However, it all boils down to one thing, *you must love yourself first, for if you love yourself sincerely, disliking and avoiding the things and actions that cause you harm will be easy*. Also when you love yourself, you will find it very easy to love, accept and tolerate everything else around you including people, animals, nature, technology and so on and so forth.

Provided your love is genuine, you would not need to try loving anything at all because your love would naturally emanate with everything you do since you would be at peace with yourself and the world. If people would be at peace with themselves like this, then conflicts and wars would never arise in the world. Finally, if you are spiritual, then you will know that your body is a temple of the spirit of God who resides within you, therefore knowing this, you would not temper with the temple of God.

2. Positive Self-Counsel (PSC):

(Becoming your own psychologist and mentor)

"Now that I know to love myself, how can I profit from my strengths successfully and fortify my weaknesses without lambasting myself and abasing my self-love and importance?" The answer to that is straightforward; whatever you do to yourself, do it with love and with the purpose of making yourself feel important (This also applies to what people may say or do against you—You receive it all with the intention and purpose to make yourself grow and progress). If you do this, you could never feel that you are being criticized because you will know that whatever the comments or opinions, they only make you a better person.

Now, of course in order to know and understand your weakness, you must analyze yourself thoroughly. And in order to transform those weaknesses into strengths or capitalize on the strengths you already possess, then you must accept, acknowledge and edify yourself unsparingly. Let us start by talking about analyzing yourself:

Self-analysis: This is more than simple introspection where you examine your mental and emotional processes. It is the way in which you can become your own psychologist; the way in which you can know exactly where you stand before you can begin to manage yourself in any way. It is the road to self-knowledge. More than just analyzing your strengths and weakness, you must analyze yourself in such a way that you will know the answers to the following questions:

"What is really important to me in my life? What do I truly love? What makes me tick or what moves me and what doesn't? What do I undoubtedly believe in? What does my heart and mind believe is my definite purpose on earth? What do I really want?"

After you have answered those questions, then you must know how you intend to get that which you want and so strongly believe is your purpose. Then with your purpose now deeply fixed in your mind, you must know clear-cut plans of how you intend to get what you want. Lastly you must know exactly what it takes to follow those plans to the letter until your objective has been achieved. If you know these things after your self-analysis, then you can be proud of yourself because it means you now know and understand yourself absolutely.

You see, knowing yourself is an important prerequisite when it comes to the art of managing oneself. *You cannot manage yourself effectively unless you know why you are the way you are.* So it is imperative that you analyze yourself truthfully without holding back anything even if some things may embarrass you. As a matter of fact, the deeper you can dig out those things that mortify you, the closer you are to self-knowledge and the easier it is to manage yourself.

Now if you find it hard to analyze yourself, you can simply ask a close member to do it with you. Or you can get into the library or internet to find books, materials and other information that can help you do it. If that too is hard for you to do, well, then you can find a professional such as a guidance and counselor, a psychologist, hypnotherapist and any other expert therapist you can think off to help. But our focus here is in managing yourself, not having other people take control over you. Besides why pay someone else a large sum of money for something you can do yourself? If you are spiritual, then you must know that the spirit that leaves in you is your guidance and counselor, all you have to do is activate it.

Self-edification: After you have analyzed and can identify who you really are, you must now become your own motivator. That is your own mentor and your own guidance and counselor so that you can turn your weaknesses into strengths and keep your strengths stronger. This is where you fire yourself with enthusiasm and inspirit yourself into taking actions that will move you closer to the ideal self—This is where you arise by yourself.

Now, there are many ways in which you can edify yourself, such as reading an artistic book, going to religious gatherings, talking to close relatives and trusted friends, listening to inspiring music, getting back in touch with nature. Or you can simply find a professional to do it for you, such as; a motivational speaker, pastor, a stand up comedian or whatever suits your personal taste. Use your ingenuity to come up with your own ideas. In order to inspire your artistry, here I am just going to share with you two methods that have always worked for me:

A) **Fictitious Mentors:** This is a method of using the imagination to edify yourself by seeking guidance, counsel, wisdom, inspiration and revelation from your chosen imaginary mentors or people that you feel can have the answers and wisdom you need. This is done by talking to them in your imagination as if they were presently there with you. You imagine the comments and answers they would give you in response to the questions you asked them.

Case in point; If your concerns are about money, you can imagine the quintessential millionaire who can advice you the way you want. If your concerns are about relationship, then imagine whoever you know that can advice you on that matter, such as a respected marriage counselor you know. If your concerns are about your health, then think about a person or doctor you know who is well versed in that field, if it is about sports or martial arts, then imagine your ideal coach or visualize the methods of your favorite athlete. If you are religious, then you can imagine, your spiritual father, mentor, prophet or The God you believe in. It all depends on YOU; what you belief, what you know, who you know and what you desire.

Keep in mind that my purpose is not to tread on your beliefs by telling you what to believe or not to believe, I am simply acting as a pointer in your path, pointing you to the concept of edifying yourself towards your desired success.

Imagination is the foundation secret in this particular method of self-edification. It requires some exercise because you have to know your chosen and imagined mentors very well. This is so that they may give you the right answers that would have come from their *REAL* personalities had they been physically there. Think of this as almost like the concept of *Arising By Falling*, in that you *take up the mind of somebody else who is above and beyond the situation you are currently in*. And that is why this exercise works because the moment you rise beyond your current negative circumstance to think about the positive things your mentors would say to you, you are in fact already above your current situation.

Now think about this; if you can arise above your adverse situations like that at will, how can you fail to overcome them? *If you can imagine the positive guidance, counsel, wisdom and inspiration that can come from other people, why can't those same revelations come directly from you?* This is indeed the nitty-gritty; the nuts and bolt of the art of *Arising By Oneself.* Make sure to think about it in your own personalized way.

In *The Art of life* book, I explain how I came about this self-edification technique while bombarded by many religious believes during my stay in Japan. I also describe the exact meditation methods I used to make this *fictitious mentors* technique be as enjoyable and as fruitful as possible. From my regular experience with this technique, if done correctly, you will receive more than just mere guidance and answers to your questions or problems; you gain the kind of discernment that will give you a gratifying experience and sustain priceless personal-revelations for your total life. I recommend this very highly

B) **Helping people when YOU need help yourself:** Another amazing way to edify yourself is to get out of your way and help people when they need help. For example, when you are down, depressed or feel worthless for some reason, by simply walking to a person in need of help and offering them the help they need can change your negative feelings in an instant and cause you to feel alive, worthy and full of purpose.

You see, *when you help somebody else, you unconsciously take your attention away from your current problems that create in you a sense of unworthiness, to feelings of self-assurance and self-worthiness that come with the ability to help somebody else.* And these new feelings you get from helping that person far outweigh your former negative feelings because unlike the former feelings, they immediately make you feel important. It is these feelings of importance that then edifies you regardless of what current problems you may have.

Tenrikyo scriptures that say, "By saving others you yourself will be saved" carry a profound truth in them because not only do their meaning relate to spiritual matters alone, they also imply to our everyday lives. Try it for yourself; the next time you feel gloomy and dejected. Force yourself to get up and find somebody else who needs help and help him or her in any way that you can. It does not matter how big or small your help for them may be, the results will be the same -- invigorating, uplifting and edifying.

Once you truly understand yourself, self-edification can help you in many beneficial ways. Such as in times when you are struggling with your inner-self or having mental blocks, emotional breakdowns, stressed-out or having any other form of minor or major depression. For example, you can use the *Fictitious Mentors* method to not only solve your problems and dilemmas, but to also find inspirations for a project you have to do at work or school. It is especially effective in times when you feel that you are in no position to be understood or helped by the people around you. The opportunities to use it, are boundless and its benefits are limitless. Try it, that you may arise by yourself!

3. Positive Self-Talk (PST):

(The power that transmutes your inspired ideas into action)

In terms of self-management, PST, or positive self-talk is exactly what it sounds like; you uplift yourself by talking to yourself positively. It is the motivational speaker in you, edifying you in precisely the way you want to be edified. For having studied yourself comprehensively, you know exactly what you need and how you need it; and PST is just that perfect tool to edify yourself the way you want.

With PST, you are in control of what messages you want inputed into you and what messages you want out, thus you can translate your weaknesses into fortitude and transform the wisdom you received from your supreme mentors into personal power. (If you are a Christian for example, you can take the scriptures from your Bible and turn them into personal confession in accordance to what you want in your life. The book of Psalms is a good way to learn how David confessed the Word of God into his life).

You see, the greatest self-power one can possess is the power to control or monitor the messages that go in and out of one's mind. Possess this power and you will possess the power to manage yourself at will. PST is the vehicle that gives you that power.

Think about it this way: Our minds receive thousands of thoughts per day . . . Thinking about this thought alone is overwhelming, therefore it is imperative that we manage ourselves by managing our thoughts. PST gives us this opportunity to manage our thoughts by controlling the words we confess to ourselves and to others.

What preys on my mind is that most of these thoughts that we receive each day are useless and we discard them as quickly as they come. Imagine how much time and energy we would conserve if we managed our thoughts economically so that we thought only the thoughts that we consciously opted for? This is why this system of self-management can have a dramatic effect if we are to apply it in our personal lives.

In other words, *by sincerely loving ourselves; positively counseling and edifying ourselves; positively talking to ourselves; tenaciously detaching ourselves from things that keep us in the past and the things that worry us in the future; and lastly by single-mindedly meditating for the sake of controlling our mind and ultimately our thoughts*; then we can dramatically change our lives for the better by limiting the useless thoughts that enter our head and also by wisely choosing the words we talk about to not only other people but ourselves.

This entire system of self-management has been scrutinized so that nothing in it is unimportant or can be left out in order for the self to be managed in its totality without partiality. But if you are, for some unfortunate reason, unable to follow the whole system to the letter, which in my personal experience is easy to apply, then I would recommend you put your attention on principles three; *PST*, and principle four; *Detachment*. Principle four is explained further in the ensuing book, *Arising by God*. To master principle three is easy and very effective if done correctly; you MUST know how to talk to yourself encouragingly.

In Botswana, if you pay attention to the words we use to speak to each other and especially against ourselves, you will not be surprised why it is so difficult for most of us, Batswana people, to grow and progress in our personal lives. Yet the country is offering us all the milk and honey we need in order to arise ourselves above our current standards.

Our poverty and failure are not because of the luck of resources or money, rather, they are a result of the words we speak to each other and most importantly to ourselves. You see most of the words we speak are words of discouragement and futility; we criticize, complain, condemn, demean and blame ourselves, others and most especially our government. We do not realize this, because rather than talk about the things that uplift us and help us grow, we instead indulge in talking about the failures of the past, the negativity instead of the good we see in our current circumstances and more sadly the fears of the unknown things we anticipate in the future.

Seriously, how can we arise and succeed if all we think and talk about is doom and destruction? This troubles me greatly about my fellow country men. We *are a peaceful, beautiful, intelligent and talented people but our **everyday-talks** are everything against what God, or nature if you will, has so generously given us?* Think about it; we have abundant natural resources like diamonds, coal and more; we are blessed with tourism from our beautiful natural environment and wildlife. Last but not least, somehow unlike most African countries we have been spared from civil wars and exploitation of our resources by our former colonizers. We even have one of the least corrupted governments in the world, yet me grumble, whine, bleat and kick up all kinds of fuss about this and that, why?

Usually these negative talks come as jokes, but then mechanical jokes can become habits and uncontrolled habits more often than not create one's reality. The principles written on the book *Arising By People* shows us how to get rid of such negative talk when dealing with people. This topic on positive self-talk is meant to complement it by doing the same thing for you. Only this time you are talking to yourself without involving other people—You are arising by *your own self*, not by people. To do so, your way of thinking must emulate the way of arising by falling. That is, you must keep yourself free from negative thoughts, emotions and actions that bring you and other people down.

Remember that in *Arising by Falling*, I said; "*When you put your attention on any negative situation, you block your mind to find a solution to arise out of it.* In other words, *when you cloud your eyes with tears over the situation you are in, you will most assuredly fail to see the next opportunity when it passes in front of you.* The best thing is to ignore or detach your emotions away from the negative circumstances before they lure you into a jeremiad over them."

In the same way, you must detach yourself from all the negativity that may bring you down by positively talking to yourself about the things that build you up instead. For instance, in order to talk to yourself fruitfully in this way; you must *audibly confess good and positive things* like; prosperity, success, achievement, victory, love, peace, happiness and whatever it is you want in your life. By the way of illustration, you can confess to yourself in this manner:

> "Good things are always happening in my life, the problems I experience only prepare me to enjoy the good things that are coming to me!"
>
> "I always accomplish my goals and in good time."
>
> "Money is coming to me in all directions and even from sources I don't think about!"
>
> "I am good at passing any interviews and speaking in public . In fact I am confident and bold when I answer interviews and speak in public!"
>
> "I always succeed, because I have the power of success within me!"
>
> "I always remember what I need to remember because I possess an excellent memory!"

The secret you must remember when making such confessions to yourself is that they must be made *audible to your ears*, *in the present tense* and *as positive as possible*. You do not want to be talking out of doubt and suggesting to yourself that you might or might not achieve that which you are confessing to yourself. This why they must be in the present tense, so that what you are saying to yourself is happening now. Another good example is in prayer: When you pray, you pray in such a way that what you pray for has already happened in the spiritual realms and you only have to take the necessary steps to receive in the natural.

When you boldly and audibly confess these things to yourself, your subconscious mind will be saturated with the optimism of the confessed words. And thus your faith will be lifted up enough to believe that what you confessed will indeed come to pass. During the time of waiting, your mind and being will remain open, alert and mindful to any opportunity that may pass by and bring you closer to the materialization of you confessions.

If you believe in Jesus for example, you can make powerful confessions in his name and not only call material blessing upon yourself but also command the spiritual realms to do as you wish. For example:

"I am free from all family curses and traditions that affected my life in the past, in Jesus' name. Thus I create a new life for myself now."

"No weapon formed against me by the enemy can prosper because I am protected by the fire of the Holy Ghost."

"My family and children are protected from all evil that try to destroy our lives now and in the future, in the mighty name of Jesus!"

"I can do all things through Christ who strengthens me, thus the task ahead of me will never be greater than the power that lives within me!"

"By the authority in Jesus's name, I command victory in my life and I win because I am the head and not the tail, above only and never beneath!"

You can even command blessings and deliverance upon yourself:

"By the blood of the lamb, I am healed in Jesus name."

"Whatever curses are blocking, my finances, my marriage and my future, I rebuke them by the authority in the name of Jesus. Be though removed and cast out into the sea!"

"By the authority in the name of Jesus, by the blood of Jesus and by power in Holy spirit, I cut myself loose from the chains and traps of my enemies."

"I can pray for every situation in my life and the lives of other believers and my prayers will be answered, in Jesus name. For greater is He that is in me than He that is in the world."

Of course you have to believe in Jesus, in order to make such confessions for without full faith in Him, then you are just confessing empty words with no possible results. Remember I am not trying to tread on your toes here, I give example using Jesus because that is where my faith is and I am not condemning any other faith either. In my life I have studied many religions and even hold two diplomas in two totally different faiths. Wherever your beliefs may be placed, be it in Buddha, Oyasama, Mohamed or Krishna, PST will work the same for you in that belief if properly applied in faith.

If you are a believer in God who wants to learn more about the realities of the spiritual things that are happening behind our earthly eyes, then I suggest and encourage you to saturate you mind with transcendental knowledge rather than waste your time engaging in sensual things that do nothing for you both in this life and the next. You can start by spending time learning about God, reading his scriptures, meditating on Him and visiting places where the real Word of God is taught. You can also watch spiritually uplifting television channels such as *Emanuel Tv* if it is easier for you that way. Yet, if you on the hand do not believe in such spiritual "mumbo-jumbo," I am not trying to convert you into anything here, I am simply opening your mind to the countless ways in which you can arise to any height of success and achievement you desire.

The fundamental tip you should take from all this is that your PST will mostly be influenced by the things you engage you thoughts and emotions in. You must analyze yourself so that you can know how to think and create your own personalized confessions according to your beliefs. Do not waste time judging my figures which are trying to guide you and miss the whole point I am pointing you at. Understand the gist of my message to you and then see how you can personalize it into your life.

Anyhow, *the most important thing in **positive self-talk** is that you talk audibly to yourself and as if the things you are confessing are happening now or have already happened in the spiritual realm*. In other words, you must believe that they have been released for you in the spiritual world and that you are currently receiving them in the physical reality by saying the right things to yourself and taking the necessary steps to attain them. Only then will you move the universe in your favor and be inspired into action to do whatever is necessary to materialize your ideas and dreams.

Jesus explained this attitude of believing and receiving clearly when he said, "*Therefore I say to you, whatever things you ask when you pray, **believe that you receive them**, and you will have them.*" That is the secret; "believing that you receive," even before physically receiving. This is the kind of believing you must have when making your positive self-talk confessions, irrespective of whether you believe in spiritual things or not.

4. Detachment:

(The art of controlling what was, what is and what will)

The reason self-management becomes too unmanageable to us at times is because we become too occupied with too many things. We want to do, have and control everything; everything in the past, in the future and in the present. We want to mix it all together and control it all, but the truth is we cannot. Human beings are made in such a way that we can only focus on one thing at time thus can only do one thing at a time. Now I am not saying it is a bad idea to multi-task, in fact multi-tasking is a good way to save time since you "kill two birds with one stone." The problem is *attachment*.

When we get attached to the things we have done in the past, the things we are doing now and the things we intend to do in the future, then we no longer multi-task because we want to save time. We do it out of a sense of urgency, greediness and anxiety. Due to these attachments, we feel the urge to hurry unnecessarily and as we do the things in haste, they become too much and they overwhelm us. Thus making it impossible to manage them. Therefore like a person standing in the middle of a flooding river, wondering whether to continue forward and cross the river or go back where he came from, you end up being swept away and drowned because you failed to act.

Also as a result of spending too much time doing random stuff unproductively, we forget ourselves in the process and fail to do the necessary things that keep us calm, composed and stately.

Things such as genuinely showing love to ourselves, guiding and counseling ourselves, talking positively to ourselves and spending some quality time with ourselves and the self alone through meditation and the like. Therefore, because we fail to notice ourselves like this, since we are only consumed by the thoughts of the things gone, the things that are and the things to be; we take risky stimulants in hopeless hopes of trying to controlling everything. The result of which we make self-management even more difficult to achieve.

The remedy to making self-management manageable is to observe and do things without attachment. *You must let go of the past you cannot change, then plan for the future without obsessing over it. You must do what you have to do now fully and fruitfully so that whatever is undone or to be done has no negative effect on your thoughts and emotions.For doing so you will know that you did the best of what you had to do when you had to do it and thus have no regrets about it.* This is the sum and substance of the art of detachment. *It frees you of the past and frees you from the future so that you are able to deal with the present without being overwhelmed by what was and what will.* Thereby leaving you with ample time and energy to take notice of your needs, wants and thus be able to manage yourself appropriately and with ease.

Detachment is the panacea that controls and manages all the regrets of what was; all the stresses of what is; and all the worries of what will.

It is one of the most important concept in all arisings for how can one arise higher if he is attached to the chains of the past? How can one focus in the now and be in the moment if he is troubled by the anxiety of the future? Attachment is the reason we fall into the illusions of the senses and thus our cosmic delusion. I elaborate further on this all-important concept in the book, *Arising By God*. Through proper understanding of it, we can know exactly what are the things that keep us attached and obsessing about things that we know are pulling and keeping us down. Make sure to give it your full concentration, consideration and contemplation.

5. Meditation:

*(The key to managing the incessant internal mental dialogue.
The gate way to the self)*

Without the practice of detachment, the mind has a lot of work to do. Unnecessary work for that matter. It begins to wander from one object of focus to another without stopping nor giving full attention to the object of focus. Because of this, we lack proper discernment and lose our memory quickly. We can hardly maintain our concentration on one particular thing and therefore making it hard to learn anything we may desire to learn. This a problem that many of us are faced with today and our modern science and medicine is doing very little to solve the problem other than through the temporary stimulants that stimulates our addiction and cause us to become even unhealthier.

Meditation is the right tool to control this incessant wandering of the mind. Unfortunately many people are skeptical of meditation. So before we go any further, let me tell you that mediation is not a cult nor a religion. If at all it is a cult or religion, it is a cult within that cult or a religion within that particular religion. By that I mean that every, cult, religion or practice has the practice of some kind of meditation in it. You see even *you* as an individual have your own unique way of meditating within your own way of doing what you do. You might not realize it but you do. This is because meditation is simply a method in which we pay attention to our thoughts in the mind and attempt to slow them down so that we can be at peace with and within ourselves.

You see with the thousands of thoughts we receive each day, if we do not find a way to slow them down, they would overwhelm us and cause us to fall into depression or go crazy. Uncontrolled thoughts is the reason why people end up resolving to acts of violence such as, suicide, murder and all kinds of sadistic destructions human beings do to the Self and to each other.

What turns people away from meditation is the idea of sitting down in a cross-legged position, appearing cross-eyed and trying to "empty the mind!" No! Mediation is not that and it is more than that. It is not about sitting down in the silence of the dark in an effort to empty the mind. It is far from that. In fact it is this "emptying of the mind" concept that many people fear because they do not understand it. They associate emptiness with darkness yet the two words have no relation. In meditation emptying the mind simply means *controlling the unceasing thoughts that rob the mind of its tranquility and rest.*

There are many forms of meditation and like I said, every one of us have our own way of meditating, regardless of whether we do it consciously or unconsciously. This is owing to the fact that all of us have our own ways and habits of finding peace and that is what meditation is; *finding peace through the constant observation of our mind.* For example, an old lady might find her peace through sitting down on her rocking chair knitting a jersey for her grand child. A man by engaging his mind in trying to fix an old car that he knows very well that it is beyond repair. Another person might while away his or her time tending to his livestock, oblivious of the afternoon sun passing on to the horizon. Other people might play chess, practice a sport, read a book, play music or cultivate their vegetable garden and tend to their flowers.

All these people will not necessarily be busy, rather than concentrate their minds on worries and problems, they prefer instead to spend time engaging their minds in focusing on some activity. Whether they know it or not, *when their attention is fully engaged, the chattering of the thoughts ceases and the mind quietens, thus they find their peace.* So you can see that it is *not* the activity that is important but the concentration that takes us away from our troubles and bring us contentment and equability when engaged in that activity. And so is proper meditation, it is not the position you are in nor the things you do in your chosen position or activity; it is the fruits of peace that are being planted in those positions or activities.

Now, the meditation I am talking about here is one that requires discipline because it is not random, it is planned; it is systematic and has been proven both by science and experience. But before I try to show you how to do it, let me give you some of its benefits so that you may understand how it can help you manage yourself:

Proper meditation controls the incessant internal chattering of our thoughts and quietens the mind. Therefore, with the mind controlled and the aimless wandering of our thoughts of the past and the future stopped; we now have enough energy and time to perceive the self, focus on self-analysis, self-edification, and thus understand ourselves completely so much that we can realize the true wisdom and potential within us. We can begin to see why we are limitless beings. Why our capacity to achieve is greater than even our ability to imagine it; and why our potential to do is beyond what our physical body can handle. Furthermore, through mediation, *we unleash our spirit to do more than just what our fear-controlled bodies and reason-controlled minds want to do*.

Now, the peace we receive from engaging on those random activities only last as long as we are absorbed in them, but *the peace that comes through trained meditation is a lasting contentment that can benefit us through out our everyday arising and falling*. That is, by virtue of meditations, we can remain content and at peace both in times of difficulties and opportunities. Far more important is the fact that *through meditation, our usually dormant sixth sense; instinct; inner voice and the subconscious mind becomes louder, clearer and more useful in our everyday life*.

Lastly, for those who believe in God, do we not spend too much time praying, requesting and confessing but spend very little time listening to the answers and presence of God? We must know that although God will speak to us anywhere and anytime, His answers will mostly come to us in our quietness, solitude and peace. Psalms chapter forty-six, verse ten says, "Be still, and know that I am God." It is no wonder that God speaks to people through dreams and visions when they are asleep, because when we are awake, we neglect the very act that gives us the chance to here from him—*Silence; Quietude and Stillness* of both mind and body! Meditation gives us all that.

There are many types of meditation out there depending on your purpose for meditating. For example, meditating for the sake of gaining good health or for the pursuit of enlightenment is different from the meditation for scholastic education or business and also different from the meditation for sports or martial arts. In the same way, meditation for religious purposes depends on your religious needs and believes. Therefore it is imperative that you know yourself and know what you want so that you can choose the right meditation technique for your needs and wants. This is why thorough self-analysis is so important.

Thus rationally speaking, because of the vastness of the meditation techniques out there and because I do not know the reasons why you want to meditate, I cannot describe to you the details in which you must meditate in this book. For those of you who have no clue what I am talking about or are seriously wanting to learn how to meditate, then I suggest you do your own due diligence and research by finding a reliable source next to your place and home. If I am next to you, feel free to contact me, it is my altruistic purpose to help anybody who wants to arise beyond their current circumstances of ignorance and dearth to those of growth, knowledge and enlightenment.

This brought me to the end of my self-management system, and like I said, do not be limited to the system described above, it is only an example of how to create your own personal way of managing yourself. Before ending the talk about this self-management system, let me add a little on a few things here to open your mind even further:

A little on fasting: Fasting is one other great tool to add to your arsenal of self-management practice. Many people misunderstand it to be a practice done by religious fanatics alone. The truth is that it is more than that and it is not to be confused with dieting either.

Fasting can be practiced by anybody willing to reap its many benefits: It is the body's way of purifying the entire system and ridding it of its toxins. It is the body's way of dealing with pain and illness—Unlike humans, wild animals use fasting to a great effect when they are unwell or hurt. You see when you stop eating for a little while, the body, especially the digestive system, has a chance to rest and thus use that reserved energy for other purposes such as healing and spiritual development. The result of which your body will be restored and your energy rejuvenated.

In terms of self-management, fasting has two major benefits; first, *it helps you bring the mind and senses under perfect control, making it easy for self-counsel and edification*. Even better, your meditation session becomes easier and smoother because with your mind and senses controlled, your thoughts are slowed and thus concentration can be achieved. Secondly, because we are not accustomed to spending too much time without food, fasting requires strong self-discipline, which when practiced, a strong will power will be developed. It is this will power which, after self-analysis, we can transmute into putting a stop to our bad habits and addictions.

For example, if we can spend a day without food, can we not spend a day without that cigarette? If we spent a day successful like that, how about two days . . . five days . . . one week . . . two weeks . . . a month? You can see from this that; ability is clearly a state of mind which is determined by one's strength of will power. *A man can do only as much as he believes he can do and if he truly believes in something, it is almost impossible for him not to do it!* It is this personal-will-power supported by a strict self-restraint that we can turn our self-management system into a habitual discipline.

Now if you believe in a higher being and want to move the heavens and the stars, then add fasting and prayer to your meditation and scriptures. Have you ever wondered why great men and women of God like Oyasama, Jesus, Buddha, Mohamed and many more fasted for so many days before being used mightily by God? There is power in fasting. But because I have opened your eyes a little about fasting, let me also touch on prayer a little:

A little on prayer: Apart from the spiritual mysteries that people believe in and get from prayer, prayer also has a psychological connotation attached to it which helps you the person in prayer to become one with your thoughts, desires and plans. Let me explain:

The minute you put your knees on the floor to pray to your God, you are saying to yourself, "I know exactly what I want. I am ready to go after it. I am ready to receive it, so God help me!" This little act alone shows you that you are not confused. So when the opportunity for getting what you wanted shows itself, you will jump to it without hesitation because through your time in prayer you have prepared your mind to see that which you need to see in order to get what you want and thus be able to act speedily yet without the confusion of haste. I am not a scientist so do your own in-depth research on this, but first listen to this with an open mind:

Prayer is the connection that takes what you have been consciously thinking about on a daily basis, into the subconscious mind which in turn ingrains those conscious thoughts into the heart of your very being. This thereby causes you to develop an unexplainable but intense desire to see your prayers turned into reality. The result of which when your desire is strong enough, you begin to believe beyond reason that what you pray for will come to pass—Faith—Hence your link with God is sealed.

How those prayers are turned into reality depends on your belief and your faith in that belief, but one thing is for certain, prayer works. Much like self-talk, if your prayers where positive, your results will be in accordance with your will, but if your prayers were negative then you can be sure to expect negative results. This is why it is so important to learn how to pray. And below is how an effective pray should be or at least look like:

First; it must start with *an expression of gratitude*; a gratitude of the things that have been, the things that you have now and a hopeful gratitude that you will indeed get what you are praying for. I talked emphatically about the magnificent effects of gratitude in the book, *Arising By People*.

Second; You must *express your purpose* in that prayer, that is your wants, needs and desires in the form of positive self-talk or positive affirmations.This is done by confirming and confessing the scriptures you believe that whatever they say will be fulfilled in your life. If you are a Christian, it is imperative that you pray in the name of Jesus because it is through him that you have the boldness to approach God. If Tenrikyo, you pray in the name of Oyasama for the same reason and if Muslim, you pray in the name of Mohamed and so on and so forth. My purpose is not teach you about religion here, that will come in my upcoming book, *Arising God; Religious Injunctions*. But keep in mind that you pray through those people because they are closer to God in spirit than you are therefore they can easily intercede for you.

Anyhow, when you pray, you must be sure to use your faith by visualizing what you pray for ultimately in your possession.

To add an icing to the cake, you must use your imagination to force yourself to believe that as you are currently on your knees praying, the spiritual force you believe in, is immediately moving circumstances; people; environment and time in your favor so that when you get up and walk, you will take the direct step that moves you towards grabbing your desires in their reality form. In other words, praying in accordance to Jesus' guidance in Mark chapter eleven verse twenty-four, which reads, "*Therefore I say to you, What things soever ye desire, when ye pray, believe that ye receive them, and ye shall have them.*"

Third; Before you get up, *give sincere gratitude again, that your prayers have been listened to, taken into consideration and acted upon.* Then smile to yourself knowing that your prayers have been answered indeed and that all your troubles are forgotten. All that you have to do is be patient, follow your heart and take daily actions towards what you prayed for. The mistake that most of us make after we pray is that after we pray we just leisurely wait and veg out on our sofas, hoping that all that we prayed for will grow legs and come running to us! It does not work like that; you must take the personal-initiative and take the necessary actions that will translate what you desired into physical reality. It is no wonder the christian scriptures say, "*Faith without deeds is dead!*"

Lastly, when you do receive what you want, be sure to *acknowledge and give gratitude to all those who have contributed to your answered prayers.* You see, all those people and things that were moved in your favor in order for your prayers to be answered, they may still need to be moved again the next time you pray. So if you do not thank and acknowledge them, what then will be moved in your favor to satisfy your ungrateful heart the next time? Most importantly, acknowledge, be grateful and glorify the one *Whom* is the real source of whatever you prayed for and received. Again, that is one of the mistakes we make after we pray; we forget where we got our blessings from and yet still expect to be given those blessing again over and over again.

Remember, *Success is much easier to achieve if you are willing to share it with other people and especially if you give them their due acknowledgement, gratitude and praise by attributing your advancement to their contribution!* How much more if you share your success with God, *THE REAL SOURCE?*

Now, of course what I write here are not definite ways in which you must follow indefinitely when you arise through prayer. Therefore be creative, open-minded and find out more on how to pray from other relevant sources. For instance, one of the more important and equally effective strategy of praying is to start by first diverting your focus from yourself to selflessly praying for others and the world around you! Remember; Under the topic we discussed earlier, *Self-edification*, I talked about how "Helping others when you yourself need help" is one of the best ways of arising higher and beyond your current unfavorable circumstances. The same works in prayer. You are most likely to receive solutions to your own prayers if pray for others before you do for yourself.

Little Quick Tricks of Self-Management:

Besides the five methods of self-management described above, there are also several other general tricks that you can use to manage yourself quickly:

*1. **Keep Things Simple.*** If you get into a house for the first time, you can easily know the wealth status of the people living in it by noticing the amount and kinds of stuff that is present in that house. The house of a poor person will be full of random and usually useless stuff lying around all over the place. On the other hand, the house of a rich person will have very few stuff in it and yet every thing you see in it will be of high quality and value.

Similarly, if you observe their minds, you will discover that a rich person, like his house, will have an organized mindset and a systematic way of doing things. The poor person, on the contrary, will be easily confused and undecided about things, touching there and there without really putting a hundred percent effort on anything. This is because the person who gets rich or successful usually always knows what he wants and goes after it with a hundred percent effort, determination and focus. The poor person does not know exactly what he wants, he wants to attain everything at once and thus gives everything a half-hearted attempt, hence the chaos in his house.

One of the reason for this distinct contradiction between these two kinds of people is this; because rich people know exactly what they want, they keep things simple and organized. On the other side, poor people are unsure of what they want and so they gather unnecessary stuff for "keepsakes." As a result of the too many stuff they keep, they become even more confused. *Simplicity is the Key*. Simplicity in a lifestyle keeps the mind simple and unclustered, making it easy to keep oneself managed at all times. Furthermore it enables one to be able to take precise and decisive decisions when necessary. So let us then think of a few ideas of how to keep things simple:

First and foremost, always know what you want, when you want it and how you want it. Secondly but equally important, do things in a systematic way so that your mind stays clear and unconfused. Then these two things being the case, when you finally do, do what you have to do, do it when you have to do it and without hesitation or procrastination. And in the doing of it, do it all completely and constructively so that there are no things left behind undone or half done.

Other more practical examples of keeping things simple are things like these: Always wash your dishes before going to bed and when you get up make sure to make up you bed and clean your room before leaving for the day. Yes, I know, this is the song mothers have been singing since the beginning of time, but their reason is well-founded; Imagine coming home from work, tired and stressed out and you enter your home only discover that your dishes are dirty and scattered all-over the kitchen? When you try to take refuge in you room, you find that your bed is full of pants, socks and towels all over it?

In addition to keeping things simple and yourself managed, keep your receipts organized but throw away unnecessary stuff such as unused boxes, papers, and so on. Keep everything where it belongs and use every object and thing for its specified use alone. Sell or give away usable things that you do not need, such, clothes, furniture and more. You get the point so what else can you think about? The biggest secret here is in keeping things simple and organized; simplicity in your house, simplicity in your office, simplicity in your car, simplicity in wallet, simplicity in everything; your relationships, your thoughts, your speech, actions, your mind, and simplicity even in our spiritual life. Simplicity is the key to clarity and order. Clarity and orderliness makes self-management all the more manageable.

2. Take Random Pauses. I talk about pausing a lot in my book because in this day and age, everybody is fighting against time and in a hurry to accumulate as much stuff on earth as they possible can. Yet while we are so busy in haste and in the middle of the rat race, we forget to breath and well, when that happens; mental malfunctions, emotional instabilities and stresses occur in our lives.

Unless we practice the art of detachment, the only way we can regain ourselves while in the middle of this fiercely competitive struggle to survive is by the means of taking *unplanned arbitrary pauses*. You see it is through taking such pauses that we can remember to stop ourselves and find time to apply the techniques we learn as we cruise along in the art of life. Without pausing, you would not even be able to learn stuff nor recognize anything that may be worthy of attention. For to learn or recognize anything, one must have the time and patience to stop and pay attention to that which can be learnt or recognized.

You see, taking pauses is not limited to big events and situation alone; you could take a random pause while in the middle of; say a speech, a deep thought, a long walk, an argument, a fight or engaged in any activity that you may find yourself in. When you do pause, breathe deeply and long then maybe focus your attention to something else such as; observing a bee hovering over a flower or watching some kids playing in the background.

If your mind is really cluttered, then maybe you could do more than shift your attention onto something else. You could engage yourself into doing a completely different activity no matter how irrelevant it is to what you were formerly doing. In fact, the more different it is from your original task that stressed your mind, the better it is for the sake of your rejuvenation. For instance, if you were busy doing some demanding homework, you could pause to join the kids to playing in the background. Or even simpler, you could go to take a cold shower instead.

As a matter of fact, while writing these books, I occasionally find myself in a point where my mind freezes and refuses to focus due to spending too much time thinking and focusing on my computer screen. So one of the tricks I play on myself is to get up and engage in a completely different activity such as practicing *Tai Chi,* and then taking a cold bath afterwards. It works like magic in rejuvenating my energy and refocusing my mind. The heaviness in my mind and body completely disappears, leaving me with enough determination and spirit to focus for many extra hours on end.

3. Change Your Habits. Now if you feel discouraged and bored to keep doing what you are doing, the technique that works for many people in countering that is to periodically change your routine and habits. Such as randomly changing your usual route to work. Erratically transforming your appearance such as changing your hair style and clothes. You could even get outside your box and unpredictably try new things such a new product, a new type of food, new sport or hobby or make new friends.

"Mmm . . . how does changing my habits and all help me with self-management?" You ask. Well, self-management is not all about forming very strict disciplines of self-control. No! In fact, do not at all confuse self-control with self-management because although self-control is a good factor to make self-management possible, they are not one thing. Self-management is about organizing your life by organizing yourself in such a way that you are happy, at peace and content within your self, with who you are and with what you do. Therefore, if changing your habits gives you some kind of peace and happiness then it is a good trick to your journey of self-management. Think about.

4. Take Timely Vacations. If all else fails, take a vacation. Taking some time off for rest or recreation and away from your usual work such as traveling to a different town or country, or going on safari is something that everybody should do. It not only gives you time for self-management, it gives you a new perspective on things and thus improves your creativity, ingenuity and resourcefulness by the time you come back to your usual routine.

Think about it this way; when you are on a long journey towards your desired destination, do you not have to stop and fill up your car with gas every once in a while? It is the same thing with the journey of life, you have to stop every so often to rejuvenate or fill yourself with the extra energy that will help take you further towards your destiny. Taking a vacation is like that. It acts like fuel and helps you fill up so that you can continue on further without the risk of getting stuck along the way.

By "timely vacations" I mean that if you are not in a position to take pauses (or vacations) whenever you want, because of work or some family obligations, then you can plan them ahead of time. In your busy schedule of life, do not forget yourself thinking you are too busy to get a vacation. For the benefit of your total well-being and the ability to keep on keeping on, taking a vacation might just be more important than the things you hold so highly in your planned schedule of life. Therefore, no matter how busy and little your time off from your regular work may be, always regard taking a planned leisurely vacation from that time to be not only a given break from work but also a necessary step to help bring you back to your obligations in tip-top mental and physical shape.

However, to be able to use your small allocated time off from work wisely, you must be able to plan and manage your time in the generality of your life in an efficient manner. In other words you must know how to balance your priorities between your work, your family and your social life. Considering how much we are always fighting against time in our modern way of life, that is no easy task but it can be done. You just need to find time and learn the esoteric art of time-management.

5. *Manage Your Time Wisely.* Time Management is a serious topic with serious implications, hence it should be given enough time for a thorough analysis and an in-depth elucidation. To do so will require either a precise book or a full chapter dedicated to it alone. Here I am just acting as an eye opener and a pointer to this pertinent factor in the art of self-management. Here then are a few pointers for you:

One, *learn about the eighty-twenty rule*; Do only the things you need to do when you need to do them by doing only twenty percent of the things that are most important first. In other words, make a daily, weekly or monthly list of the things need to do in that allocated space and time. Classify or enumerate the thing in accordance to their importance, starting with the most important at the top. Then in that list choose to do the first twenty percent of things cataloged.

Two, *keep it at the back of your head that action eliminates fear*; If some of the things you need to do are either too difficult, too scary or too demanding, then you can rectify your fear of them by acting upon them without hesitation first and with speed. You see, when you delay to act because you are afraid, you only magnify your fear and push yourself further and further away from doing what you had to do. I shall talk about this further under *The Art Of Success*, a topic coming later on.

Three, *always stay organized*; Talking about being organized takes us back to the idea of keeping things simply. But in simple, the trick to keeping things simple and staying organized is in your ability to do things systematically. Therefore, if you want to master yourself by managing your time wisely, then you must learn to do things in a systematic way. In other words, be methodical in your doings, pause and plan before you act; find out the right and wrong way of doing what you have to do before you do it then strictly do it in the correct manner that it has to be done. I tell you, do things in this specified way and you will save yourself a lot of time. And with enough time in your hands, self-management will become an effortless habit that you will enthusiastically enjoy.

Finally, *possess knowledge, be self-analyzed, develop self-control and set your priorities straight*! In explanation; you must know what you need to know about your field and know yourself that you may have the self-confidence to stand your ground. Then you will be able do what your have to do without the hesitation caused by the random external influence of other people's opinions about your situation. With a developed self-confidence and poise, you can then have your priorities straight and know not to make promises you know you will not keep. In other words, you will know when to accept other people's responsibilities over your own and when not to; when to say, "Yes" and when to say, "No!"

So Then, How Do I Know That I Need To Manage Myself?

Well, self-management is an introspection; a self-examination; and a soul-search that everybody *must* do everyday. The reason is because everyday there is dust that enters and clouds our minds; impurities that enter and destroy our bodies; and delusions that block our spiritual advancement. Therefore everyday we must take care to be mindful of the external things that can dirty our minds, weaken our bodies and sell our souls into ignorance and destruction.

This can be done through, self-observation, contemplation and the application of the *Self-Management System* described above, but not limited to it. Through the above system or your own personalized system, we can attain a self-awareness that enables us to recognize the *toxic* signs of *Falling By Arising* and *The Futile Artifices of Falling By People* (as described in the book, Arisings). It is when we recognize these signs that we can be sure that it is time to manage our lives by managing ourselves.

To make it easier for you, below is a checklist of the toxic signs that you can use to discover your own **Checklist of Self-Management**. That is, are you having, doing or experiencing the following noxious signs:

- *Depressing thoughts that start to occupy your mind?*
- *Behaving like a Maudlin Man who is foolishly sentimental?*
- *Stealing your existence away through the tricks of procrastination?*
- *Starting to find life meaningless and everything else pointless?*
- *Repressed by the oppressing thoughts of depression?*
- *Obsessed about your own self-importance and false pride?*
- *Showing too much vanity, narcissism and egocentrism?*
- *Talking about yourself incessantly, rather than listen to others?*
- *Interrupting people in order to talk about your own selfish ideas?*
- *Impatient with people, especially your own family and children?*
- *Overly criticizing, condemning, complaining and blaming others?*
- *Failing to give gratitude, appreciation and credit to others?*
- *Having too many negative emotions of lust, anger, hatred etc?*
- *Controlled by fear, lack of forgiveness and vengefulness?*
- *Being unreasonably anxious, suspicious, mistrustful—Paranoid?*
- *Tormented by doubt, disbelief and spiritually frustrated?*

If you find any of the above poisonous signs of falling then it is time to **pause** your busy life and give yourself some *quality time of Self-Management* and take care of yourself before you destroy your life and the life of others. You see these negative signs will not only harm and destroy you, they will harm and destroy other people around you because they are, as a matter of fact, *very contagious. Like yawning, those who see them in you may find themselves doing the very thing that they hated in you, that is if their internal make up is not strong enough to resist the influence.*

Please continue to remember that I am not teaching you anything here for there are many ways in which you can manage yourself effectively; it all depends on the knowledge of yourself and your situation. I only open your mind to the idea of self-management so that you can discover how to apply it into your personal art of life and arise yourself above your current problematic situations to any desired end you may choose.

Before closing, permit me to share with you what I call the **Management Truth of the Millennium:**

When it comes to management*, we cannot always manage everything in our lives nor always be in a position to manage our environment, but the one thing we can ALWAYS manage is our own inner-selves*. That is, we can manage the *internal-make-up* which influences the decisions and choices we take for our lives. I will describe these things in detail later in *The Mathematics Of Life*. But in short:

We cannot always control or avoid what happens to us, but we can always control our reactions to what happened and happens to us!

Having managed and mastered ourselves, we can then be in a position to try and manage or control our environment, other people, our nation and finally the world. It is only through this self-control and self-mastery which comes through self-management that the world can follow our lead, trust our judgements and pursue our standards. This is the **management truth of the millennium**, there is no greater self-governing truth than it. If you want to become a *world-class* leader, then *Think About It Possessively And Run With It.*

ARISING BY THE ARTISTIC LIFE

"*A*rt *is long, life is short: There is so much knowledge to acquire, that a lifetime is not sufficient.*" This is one of my favorite proverbs because the truth in it is so profound that it inspired me to write about the art of life, by comparing life with a work of art. You see, there is an art in everything, because in everything there is a way of doing that thing. The same way there is a way to hold a spoon or hold a knife, there is a way to walk, talk, work, and there is a way to live life. And in this way there is an art in which if you can learn or create your own so that life becomes easier and more interesting to live.

Now *a man is as creative as he thinks he is and as capable as he believes to be. He can do ONLY what he thinks he can do and if he truly believes in something it is almost impossible for him not to do it.* By his artistic ability a man can get out of any situation that he may find himself in. It all purely depends on how creative his mind is or willing to be. And since creativity is the art of the mind and all men have a mind then all men are creative. Therefore if all men are creative then all men are artistic enough to understand the art of life and arise by it.

That being so, one should never be disappointed or moved by the bad strokes in life because all works of art are bound to have mistakes and the artist's apron is sure to get some stains. Instead one should look at the bad strokes as not only learning curves but also additions to the uniqueness and originality one's own picture. I mean, have you ever seen an artist who gets bothered by the fact that he gets his aprons dirty while he paints? Never, right? In the same way, we should life like we are its artist, so the mistakes or spills we make along the way are all just unavoidable processes that are bound to happen. All real artist know this, hence they are not bothered about how much they get their apron's dirty as they work.

Below then is how I see myself as an artist of life, hopefully it will inspire you to discover the real artist hidden or dormant within you:

The Art Of Life:

Art is simply the man's creative skills in the faculty of the mind and imagination expressed into physical beauty. Life is the canvas in which he can practice the application of these skills using the tools given to him in his present time and environment. The tools of man vary in accordance to many things; his heredity, the environment he is in and the natural resources in that environment. But the greatest tools he possess are with him, within him and controlled by him always. That is, his mental attitude towards what he intends to do or not do with his canvas, the thoughts that dominate his being on an everyday bases and the ideas which he takes either seriously or for granted.

My soul acts like my paints of many colors. My mind holds the vision necessary to create the finished work, my body and hands make physical use of the paint-brush. Life is my canvas and the spirit provides the energy needed to produce the work. My conscience leads, corrects and guides me. And my God and wisdom are like the apron that protects me from the unexpected spills and mistakes that come in the same package as doing the art work. With all these things at my finger tips, I, AM, no doubt An Artist of Life! What more do I need to ask and pray for? What more do I need to start creating my destiny; the picture of my life; the picture of my dreams—My heart's desires?

You see, just as the brush is useless without the paint and the canvas, the paint useless without the canvas and the brush, the canvas useless without the brush and the paint. The mind, body and soul must be continually present and work as one in order to help one live a full and rewarding life. In other words, My physical health is just as important as both my mental and spiritual health. To live completely without too many problems in my life's journey, I must take care of all aspects of my being as a human being. A sound mind, a live soul, an active spirit and a healthy body are most crucial to attaining success and a gratifying life. Everything else like material possessions are unnecessary excess.

A special painting is one that is unique and original. In the same way my life should not be a portrait of someone else. I should discover myself, my skills, my talents and my character and arise by them without trying to copy some famous person I saw on television. The trick is to always remember that every person is original, unique and special in their own god-given way. The unique differences in us; in our personalities or appearances should be our most cherished traits.

Great artists are originators of their own sketches and they always follow through to finish their own painting. I ought to start my own work and do it completely and constructively without waiting to be told so or lingering around to start on somebody else's initiative. The secret is to trust in my own abilities; my own talent and capacity to perform greatly. Depending on the work of other men or waiting to be first encouraged and approved by others limits our potential to achieve for it inhibits our creative faculty of the mind to do its job. Therefore, I do not wait to get inspired others or learn from they if they won't teach me. I dig deep within myself and get inspired to take the personal-initiative. If I am not able to ignite the creative fire within me by myself, nature is there to inspire me, all I need to do is just reach out to him.

If I find it in my heart and mind to have a picture, I must start painting it, imagining a picture will not bring about the actuality of that picture in my canvas. If I find it in my heart and mind to have wealth I must start working towards it, hoping, dreaming, fantasizing nor planning will not bring about the results I want— Success requires action. Many people spend a good part of their life wasting their energy thinking, "I wish I were that . . . !" "I hope I can get that . . . " Yet by the time they wake up from their day-dreaming, they are already either to old and weak to do what they could have done years back. Or simply, the opportunity has passed them by. As for me, my dreams and goals are not controlled by the mediocre norms society has placed upon us; whatever I want, as long as I know that it is achievable, it is right and that it will not hurt me or others, then I go after it definite focus no matter what "they" say.

The hardest thing in art is knowing the first line to paint and life is the same way; the hardest thing in life is knowing what I want, what to do about it and in what direction I must take my life. Once I know the answers to the above questions then life becomes easy and pleasant. If you are confused about what you want in your life, take out a pen and paper, write down all the ideas you have. List down all your weaknesses and strengths, jot down all the pros and cons of those ideas, in other words, *analyze yourself.* Then make a precise plan of how to go about it all and finally take a decisive action towards your goal. *Action eliminates fear.* The cure to my inability to start anything lies in my capacity to take personal-initiative and act without hesitation against my fears. Put in a simple manner; when I am afraid or do not where or how to begin, I just start from anywhere and anyhow!

The way I can foresee my painting is the same way I can foresee my future life, therefore just like I prepare my brushes, paints and sketches for my final painting in my head, I must also prepare for my future by thinking about my ideas, writing down my plans and taking decisive actions in my life. But I should remember that the final picture does not use the same amount of paint as the sketches, so I too must be realistic in my preparations and also realize that life requires more than planning and taking actions; I must sincerely have faith and believe that that which is in the future will surely come to pass. As in art, using the imagination faculty of the mind is vital to the process of translating our ideas and visions into their physical equivalent.

In order to draw or paint a straight line I must look ahead of my brush. And so is life; in order to live a rewarding life, I ought to see the big picture by clearly seeing and making plans into my future, *not* by living in the past, nor by getting side tracked by the adversities that accompany life. A runner that looks behind as he runs loses his speed, if want to progress further and faster in my life, I have got to let bygones be bygones. I have got to remember that:

Whatever happened, happened,
Whatever happens now is happening,
Whatever may happen, may or may not happen,
The problems of the yesteryear are my lessons of today.
The mistakes of today do not become the habits of tomorrow.
Thus let it all be and be, for only then will I be at peace.
Everyday is a new day—A new era in my life.
Learn to accept, forgive and let go.
Let it all be and be free!

Only the artist owner can vividly see the mental image of the final painting he intends to create in his head, no other artist can advice him otherwise, unless he has the supernatural power to enter into his brain. In much the same way, the opinions of other men are irrelevant to my success unless they can vividly see and understand my purpose and what I intend to create and how I intend to create it. Like a tea-lover surfs his tea to make sure he drinks only what is smooth and clean, I too must surf the free flowing opinions of other men who may falsely think that they know what is best for me.

Just like I must imagine a big painting as a finished product in my mind but start by making small sketches of it, it is essential that I dream big but start small. Like the common saying, "Rome was not built in one day," most human beings have yet to reach the spiritual stage where they can easily materialize their desires at will and in an instant. We must work our way towards the realization of our mental goals step by step and in a systematic way (see the upcoming chapter on *The Mathematics of Success* for further details).

A finished picture must come out from an empty canvas, something must come out of nothing. So why should I worry when I have nothing or no capital to start with in my life? The world we see was created from the nothing we do not see and in the same way, the development, infrastructure and technologies we see today came from the ideas that were not seen. Stop worrying about what you do not have and do not wait to possess something in order to start possessing other things—Possessions come from nothingness. Think about this artistically!

If I want a beautiful painting, I have got to expect and accept a few drops of paint on my clothes as I paint, but then again I can always put on an apron or buy new clothing. And so is life, I must take risks and accept a few problems along the way, but if the problems persist, I can use, like an apron, the ways and laws in which one can achieve success. For instance, I can arise by falling or arise by people, arise by God or simply arise by myself. The opportunities to arise are limitless. Remember, life necessitates adversities and problems as necessary ingredients to its attainment. If you are afraid to get your clothes when painting the destiny of your life, you will never go far nor let alone be able to start.

The very same way that I do not think about cleaning my apron before finishing the painting, I should not criticize my small beginnings before I even get close to achieving my final goal. Finish first, criticize later because everything in life has something in it to criticize, therefore if you criticize every little mistake or problem you see you will never be able to finish your work. This does not apply to criticizing yourself alone, criticizing others can also have futile effect to your own work as more energy and time will be spent criticizing rather than creating! You see, criticism and creativity can never live in the same mind.

A line painted by mistake brings with it its own unique style to it, thus making the art piece to be more distinctive and original. In much the same way I let my mistakes and difficulties bring me closer to an abundance of life experiences and wisdom. In other words, I turn adversities into advantages—I arise by falling—I adapt, improvise and overcome any obstacle on my way to freedom by turning it into a ladder that I can use to climb higher to the skies of my success and freedom.

Not every line drawn by mistake can be erased, sometimes I need to simply paint over it and forget. And so is life; Not everything in my past can be good or easily forgotten, occasionally I need to accept it, learn from it, let it go and move on to bigger and better things. Living in the past only encourages stagnancy and failure because death, poverty and sorrow regresses backwards while life, success and happiness progresses ahead. Therefore, in lingering around in the past, you will not find the bright life you are looking for other than sorrow, disappointments and ultimately death. Life is found only in the vehicles that move forward.

A good painting cannot be unless the brush that creates it first becomes unclean. My hands must get dirty in order to produce anything in my life. You see, to create for myself the opportunities of a white collar job, I must not undermine the importance of doing the blue-collar job as a stepping-stone to my desired goal. Life favors those who are not choosy and do not mind getting their hands dirty.

An Artist is never bored by his work unless he has no interest in it. Boredom is caused by lack of interest. Where there is interest, boredom cannot be found. So whenever you find yourself bored and unenthusiastic, simply look for something that can awaken my interest in whatever it is you would be doing. For example, rather than indulging your attention on the things you do not like, look for the positive and interesting things in that seemingly boring situation or thing.

An artist paints out of interest not just mere talent for without interest the artwork will be worse off not painted. In the same way the secret to a good life is having the interest to live it. Interest in work will almost always beat talent. And if you think that you have no talent, you can develop it by first developing interest. But if you find that your talent is not producing fruit, then you water it by arousing your interest in it. You see, a living man without the interest in life invites death and a dying man with a lively interest in life encourages life and evades death. Think about it?

People can destroy my painting but they cannot destroy the image I have of it in my head. In life, people may rob me of my material possessions, but never of the ideas that created those possessions. So despite all the discouragement and criticism I may get from people, I must keep on dreaming and keep on keeping on. I must never be discouraged if people spit on my small beginnings but holdfast to the ideas and dreams in my head. You see, a financially rich man without ideas is in fact poor tomorrow, but a financially poor man with good ideas is indeed both rich today and tomorrow. It is best to guard my unseen ideas than to spend time protecting the physical possessions that everybody can see.

Patience is the life behind art. Art is the creativity behind life. So is life; I need to be patient to produce a presentable piece of work; without it, to see my work through, I might as well quit today. Without the patience to watch the dreams in my life manifest and my destiny unfold, I might as well die today. And while I wait patiently, I have got to be artistic in order to live a creative and enjoyable life. If I do not add color to my lifestyle nobody will do it for me because everybody has his own life to paint. There is a contemporary saying in my language, "Monate o a itirelwa," which simply means if you want to party or enjoy life, you have got to go where the festivities are, the pleasures will not come to you! But if you cannot go or find them, be creative wherever you are and the pleasures will come to you.

A painter never procrastinates his painting because he knows that everything will dry up; the brushes will dry up and the paints will not mix up well. In the same way, a go-getter will not drag his feet to success because he knows that procrastination is not only a thief of time, it is a thief of life. There is no such thing as waiting for "perfect timing" because every moment in life is in it its own perfect time, the only thing we can wait for is dearth and death. When we wait, all our driving energy, motivation and the work we have already done begins to dry up. Such that by the time we have recovered our full energy and motivation, life will have already passed us by like the wind and we would then have to start the painting from the beginning. Worse off, we may not be able to find the resources that contributed to our initial work. Even worse than that, when we idle and procrastinate, the fear that block people from beginning stuff begins to grow.

An earnest painter finishes his paintings. A serious human being takes nothing for granted, leaves nothing behind and lives a life of no regrets because he knows that unfinished business is like a bush thorn in your back pocket, it never allows you to sit down and relax. Moreover, it will not only haunt you to the end of your current life but also continue to do so in your after-life and thus prolonging your chances of ending the cycle of rebirth, that is, if that is your belief. Below is a vivid poem about this from the book *Arisings*:

> *"A little break, a little nap, a little talk,*
> *Maybe a little fun before I get to work," he says.*
> *But before he knows it, poverty attacks him in his sleep,*
> *Scarcity robs him till he screams and bleeds!*

"Tomorrow, what great work I will have done . . .
What a great man I will become after I do the job," he thinks.
But now on his deathbed he lies, having done none,
With his mind full of regrets; in his ship of depression he sinks.

His thoughts tell him; "You are fading from the globe
And nobody is watching nor noticing.
All you left for your children is a mountain full of hope,
A hope of things you intended to do in the offing."

"But it is not my fault," he comforts himself.
"I waited and hoped that tomorrow I would have overcame."
Yet now he is all alone with nobody to blame but himself,
Because things always change so his tomorrow never came.

A clever artist always takes a break, pauses and takes a step back in order to review his work, renew his energy, refocus and see his picture from a distant because only from far can he clearly see his work as whole. In my busy work life, I always make sure to take a holiday break in order to smell the flowers and breathe some fresh air somewhere in a place like the *Okavango Delta*. By doing this, I can be far in enough to have the vision of the big picture in a good perspective for its re-evaluation. Then when I Come back my mind will be freshened to think clearly and see problems from a different perspective and my energy renewed and ready to work again. Taking breaks and pauses like this is very important especially in a modern lifestyle, make sure to think about it strategically.

The reward of a well done painting is in seeing its finished product and being satisfied with the result of the effort put in it. And so is life; the reward of a well lived life is in lying down in my death bed looking forward excitedly to my next phase of existence, having no regrets of the past, knowing that I finished all that I started and did the best of all that I could possibly have done. Always do what you have to do when you have to do it so that you will not have to worry about it when you do not have to. This is my quotidian philosophy of life.

If an artist is not satisfied with his final painting, he does not crumple it with his hands or throw it away into a trash can, because he knows the time, sweat and energy he put into it. If I fail at something, I do not beat myself down and fall into depression or develop suicidal thoughts. Instead I commend myself for having tried and then lift my head up to try something else or find another way of doing it over again. If the road is muddy I do not quit and go back, rather I put on some protective boots and cross over.

If my body gets injured or dies in the process, then I can turn that injury to my advantage by doing something that I could not have done or would not have done otherwise with a healthy body. And as for death, I see it as an opportunity in which my soul can move on to a better place or find a new, healthier and better body to continue on the progress of my purpose in the next life with a new body. This is of course in accordance to one's spiritual believes. Some may just believe that the spirit throws away it's limiting body to find its suitable place in the spiritual realms. Whatever the beliefs, every situation has in it, its own unique way of arising from it.

Just like art chooses its artist, a good painting sells itself. A good character finds its own good opportunities in life even where education cannot find. For example, through out most of my schooling years, my mother and I barely had enough money to pay for my education. But while many other students were suspended from school because they did not pay their school fees, I on the other hand was allowed to continue my education without pay. Why? Did I have some kind of special witch-craft or favor with the owners of the school? No, it was in fact my character which paid my school fees. And this to me has been proof throughout my life that character is worth more than money and paper certificates.

A painting is a result of vision, believe, hard-work and endurance. Action or work supported by commitment, courage and patience with believe, is the key to transmuting my vision into reality and thus producing success and happiness in my life. There are many shortcuts to many things in life, but there is no shortcut to hard-work, even money cannot substitute hard-work because to make that money you had to work for it first. Anything that has not been worked for has a very short lifespan because the skill that it requires to maintain it can only be gained in the experience that it took while woking for it.

A finished painting, required some initial capital, and the capital you put into the painting is what determined the quality and quantity of the final picture. That is, how much paint you use and how big you want your picture to be in your chosen size of canvas determines the final prize of your product. In the same way, the income I receive in my life depends on the education, money, movable assets and energy input I contribute to my chosen line of work or business. I cannot think and contribute small then expect to achieve big. I cannot belittle people and expect them to respect me. There are so certain laws of nature that we must obey and follow in order to accomplish certain things we desire.

Every Artist dips his brush in his own soul and paints his own nature into his pictures. I make up my life by the very essence that is deep within my being, which means that what and who I am affects the outcome of my life picture. Yet what I do is as a result of what I think, and what I think a product of my environment and the opinions of people I allow to influence me. But no opinion or environment can affect me without my allowing it to do so. Self-management which goes hand in hand with self-mastery, is necessary part in producing the final product of what I am or who I am to become.

Art without the Artist is hopeless, the Artist without the Art is meaningless, for the Creator is only the Creator through his Creation, without his Creation the Creator is meaningless and without the Creator, the Creation is hopeless. And so are many things in life including God. Everything in nature and in life is interrelated. Teamwork, harmony and peace in the workings of our relationships, ideas and even "the self" is imperative to not the success of each individual but also to the progress of human kind. Without "this" how can I understand "that?" Without "that" how can I comprehend "this?" You see it is through uncritical comparison among us and things that we can grasp and make sense of things as they are. Think about this seriously.

In conclusion, I can say that an artist is a person who looks for challenges and proves them doable in his canvas of life. And the artist never fails to overcome the challenges because if he is unable to replicate exactly what he sees in front of him, he has the option to pick up his brush and contort what lines he fails to make straight into his own unique and appealing style. In the same, whatever needs to be done and can be done in life, do not run away from it, "JUST DO IT!" If in your life you meet:

> *A piece of information, make sure to learn about it,*
> *A brilliant idea, take action and materialize it,*
> *A complex math problem, challenge it,*
> *A beautiful piece of art, admire it,*
> *A lovely flower, stop n smell it,*
> *A plaything, play with it,*
> *A tasty fruit, enjoy it,*
> *A gift, receive it,*
> *A dream, be it,*
> *A debt pay it,*
> *A race, join it,*
> *A fight, avoid it,*
> *A pit, jump over it,*
> *An obstacle, remove it,*
> *A bewilderment, untangle it,*
> *A difficult predicament, solve it,*
> *A child deprived of basic needs, give it,*
> *A blessing wrapped with problems, unwrap it,*
> *A bad situation too mystifying to change, pray about it!*

Let me leave you with this artistic thought from Bruce Lee; "*Art lives where absolute freedom is, because where it is not, there can be no creativity.*" There is nothing impossible for an artistic mind to accomplish. If you find yourself in what seems like an impossible situation, simply open your mind and think artistically, "What would an artist do in this situation?" "Would he paint over the problem lines?" Or "Would he add his unique style to the problem lines?" Or maybe "He will simply contort the difficult lines to his advantage?"

"What would an artist do?" If your country gives you the democratic freedom to be yourself and do what you want when you want and how you want it, why not do the same for your mind—The freedom to be creative; original, unique, imaginative, inventive and ingenious?

ARISING BY THE ART OF SUCCESS

In my perpetual search for wisdom and knowledge of the phenomenon, I have discovered that success is easily attainable to anyone who understands and follows the laws and principles of nature. And that these laws or principles have been pre-set since the beginning of time and do not change with time. They have never changed and will never change because they do not change. Even the Almighty himself, although he is above these laws which he created at the time of creation, he is bound by these laws!

For example, God will not give a lazy man riches. Instead if the lazy man acquires riches through inheritance and continues to be lazy, those riches will be taken away from him! But if the lazy man decides to stop his laziness and starts to work hard, then only then can he maintain those riches. So you see if God also works through these principles or laws of nature how much more should we learn about them and apply them into our personal lifestyles?

These laws produce a cycle of failure or success depending on how you use them. They are like a circle without a circumference; like yin and yang. They are limitless and without bound but can be used and applied to even to our smallest mundane daily activity. They complement and implement each other yet they exist on their own and can be used separately. We all know these laws, they are free to use and are available to anybody, anywhere and at any time.

That said, although I personally depend on God for the salvation of my soul, I do not depend on the stars, the gods, fate or luck and even

God himself in order to achieve any of my earthly dreams and desires. Why? Because as human beings we have been given everything including the mental, physical, people and natural resources to get us where we desire to go in this current life. To top it up, we have been given these pre-set laws of nature to help us utilize those resources.

Therefore I can boldly say that I do not depend on the gods to go through this life. I pioneer my own path by studying and implement the god-given laws of nature to create success and achievement in my own life. When I do enquire God by prayer and faith, I support that prayer and faith by taking physical actions that enable me to implement and apply these unfailing laws. The same way that I can see a finished painting in my mind's eye and paint it exactly the way I see it, is the same way that I can create my own success with these laws. I do not wait for luck because luck is for the lazy and indecisive:

You see;
Luck Requires Action, Action Eliminates Fear, Fear
Handicaps Success, Success Appreciates Speed. Speed Seizes
Opportunity, Opportunity Likes Preparation, Preparation Needs
Proper Planning, Planning Demands Strict-Discipline, Discipline
Supports Persistence, Persistence Befriends Purpose. Purpose
Rises From Desires, Desires Are Born From Ideas.
Ideas Depend On Self-Motivation, Motivation Affects
Your Lifestyle, Lifestyle Dictates Your Destiny.

Destiny is Created by Commitments,
Commitments Come from Daily Decisions
Daily Decisions follow Personal-Initiative,
Personal-Initiative Turns Ideas Into Money! Money
transmutes Desires Into Dreams.

Dreams Turn Poverty Into Success,
And Success Favors The Risk-Takers,
Risk-Taking Involves Unshakable Courage,
And Courage Does Not Wait For Favorable Luck,
Because Luck is Hopeless Without Courageous Action.

. . . And so the gentle Cycle of Success Continues:
Action Eliminates Fear, Fear Handicaps Success, Success
Appreciates Speed and Speed Seizes Opportunity: Those who depend

on luck are lazy because they lack the most essential ingredient of success; *Personal Initiative*. Like hope and faith, luck requires one to take the first step and make the necessary plans of action that lead him in the progress of success. But since success is hindered by fear, I conquer the fear of being a beginner and the fear of failure by taking immediate action before the fear rises above my throat and drowns me in the depths of poverty and failure.

Then I must act fast because time disappears like a roll of toilet paper so I must use it wisely. Otherwise if I unfold it mindlessly, without realizing it, I would be left with nothing, but regrets of things that could have been. You see, the rapidity with which I attain what I want depends on the initiative, speed and the courage with which I use the time and resources that are available to me in that environment. For example, when my friends were teaching me gymnastics tricks at *White Lotus Marital Arts Center*, I always countered my fears by mentally repeating this positive self-talk to myself, *"Action eliminates fear!"* And it worked like magic. So you too can turn these laws into positive self-talk whenever you meet some crisis in your life—All you have to do is choose a law that suits your situation at that particular moment.

Opportunity Likes Preparation, Preparation Needs Proper Planning, Planning Demands Strict-Discipline, Discipline Supports Persistence, Persistence Befriends Purpose.

Every time I fail to make plans for my goals I find that I fail to attain them. Yet every time I take the time to make the necessary preparations I almost always succeed to accomplish my plans unless of course I made false plans. This is why when making plans I must make sure that I do not lose my patience and discipline in doing so because making wrong plans can mean creating wrong calculations when the opportunity comes. Making wrong plans they can also cloud my eyes and mind and cause me to expect a different opportunity when the right opportunity is passing right before my eyes.

You see, the more readily I have prepared, the quicker I am able grab any opportunity when it avails itself. And yet again, when an opportunity finds me prepared and ready to go, I find that I do not hesitate and waste any time by being indecisive because my mind would already be made up and unconfused! This proves that speed is truly essential for success. It is imperative thus, that I make sure that I prepare well in advance and plan wisely so that my mind remains clear and unconfused about what I really want. This is because when an opportunity comes, I must know exactly what I want otherwise I would be unable to act appropriately and in good time.

Now, if my goals require no necessary planning, it is still advisable to take my time . . . **pause**, breathe and contemplate about the opportunity that is about to come because doing so will also enable my mind to act faster and with clear conscience when the opportunity arrives. Simply taking in a deep breath and breathing out slowly and long before taking immediate action can do wonders in the way I will react and behave in that current opportunity. This is because *pausing* also acts like good planning and preparation by keeping my mind focused, clear and unconfused thereby causing me to be fast and decisive in my actions.

Although we may be given the laws of success to help us achieve it, life is not always easy. Sometimes in order to make our plans come to pass we must fight and endure the hardships and adversities that it takes to see our plans come to pass and achieve our desired success. Hence I must be self-controlled and poised in order to manage the thoughts and emotions that may arise as a result of the adversities and also be disciplined enough to avoid being side-tracked by the many distractions along the way. However, no man can have a strong enough persistence to carry his plans through unless he has the self-discipline to do so. In other words, in order to achieve my purpose, I must have the persistence to follow through and that kind of persistence entails that I develop very strict self-control and discipline.

Discipline is especially essential for those men and women who are their own boss or anybody who works at home or without somebody else aside to push them to finish the work. Without discipline the student can cannot finish his homework or study sufficiently for his exams. Without discipline the athlete cannot spend long hours of sweat and muscle aches training for his competitions. Without discipline, the President, cannot wake up early everyday to read newspapers and learn about what is going on in his country.

You see, it is because of discipline that I was able to follow my plans of working eight hours a day as if I had a regular job, in order to finish writing my books. Without the strict self-discipline to follow my plans through, I would never have had the persistence to follow and organize my ideas for the books. You see discipline gave me the persistence to endure all the adversities that came with writing this book, such as the computer crashing half-way through and losing all my notes. Or simply the discipline to force myself to wake up early in the morning and sleep late at night writing, writing and writing!

> *Purpose Rises From Desires, Desires Are Born From Ideas.*
> *Ideas Depend On Self-Motivation, Motivation Affects*
> *Your Lifestyle, Lifestyle Dictates Your Destiny.*

To discipline oneself requires a significant amount of strong will which is influenced by an intense purpose deep-seated in the heart of the very being that causes all men to have wants. It is deep-rooted in the heart of hearts. This purpose is sustained and driven by an intense desire to see the man's idea become physical reality. It is in fact the man's intense or burning desire that translates into a purpose to see the ideas become a reality. However, before the desires existed, they were only mere ideas in the head, but when those ideas were taken serious, chewed on and liked, they became desires which later became a purpose to see them turn into reality.

Frankly speaking, an ignored idea could be the difference between life and death in that particular person or other people's lives. The single most important possession that every human being has and which it can never be taken away by anything or anyone is an IDEA! As a society we must cherish all our ideas and never underestimate anybody who comes to us with an idea no matter how many signs of poverty or illiteracy we may see in that person's appearance. You see, *everything in life started from nothingness and ideas are the only commodities that exist in nothingness.* They are the evidence that all reality we see comes from nothing we see with our physical senses. They are the substance of things we hope to do and the dreams we have in our hearts.

Yes, everything begins with an idea, but how we come up with those ideas is greatly motivated by the external and internal influences affect us in our daily lives. These influences come from our environment and the people around us but later affect and shape our lifestyle. Then with the same repetitious lifestyle or way in which we live our day to day life, our destiny is formed. Therefore in simply, take your ideas serious for they may form your desires; the desires which may later become your purpose and the purpose which may affect your lifestyle and create your destiny.

In my case, one of the secret to the reason why people think that I am creative is that I never ever throw away or take for granted any idea that enters my mind no matter how small or silly it may be. As a result I always have numerous ideas coming out from my head and mouth as words of wisdom or creativity. In fact if I think the idea to be too small or too silly, I write it down and store it down somewhere in case I may need it in the future. But if I find that the idea can be of some use to me, I not only write it down but I also keep it at the back of my head. Depending on how valuable it may seem, I run it through my head several times until that idea becomes a vivid picture in my mind's eye. Then if I like that image, I let it turn into an ardent desire which I ultimately mold it into a clear purpose followed by persistent plans to see it turn into physical form.

In reality, that seemingly useless idea could be what initiates my arising or falling in the art of life. It could be the difference between gaining success or poverty; happiness or misery and dissatisfaction or contentment.

Destiny is Created by Commitments,
Commitments Come from Daily Decisions
Daily Decisions follow Personal-Initiative,
Personal-Initiative Turns Ideas Into Money! Money
transmutes Desires Into Dreams.

Now of course I will not realize my destiny by simply living any lifestyle society or random influences choose for me. I must make decisive decisions to make definite commitments that will bring my lifestyle in line with what I believe to be my destiny. Nobody can make such decisions and commitments for me, I must take the personal-initiative to take the necessary steps that will bring closer to achieving my dreams and realizing my destiny. Keep in mind also that these decision are not a one time decisive that that, "I have now decided to become rich," they are decisive actions I have to make every single day with the awareness that they are leading me towards what I desire.

For example if money (or any material possession) is what YOU desire, sitting around and airily wishing for it will not bring it to you, you must take the initiative to do all that you need to do in order to bring it to you. And as will be explained later in the chapter, *Arising By The Art of Financial Freedom*, money is the commodity that will help you transmute your ideas and desires into the physical reality you dream about.

> *Dreams Turn Poverty Into Success,*
> *And Success Favors The Risk-Takers,*
> *Risk-Taking Involves Unshakable Courage,*
> *And Courage Does Not Wait For Favorable Luck,*
> *Because Luck is Hopeless Without Courageous Action.*

In the journey towards success, one of the most typical and common stumbling blocks that stops people from achieving is fear. I talk about fear a lot in my books, but that is because it is worth exposing it. It is the fear of taking risks that shutters most people's dreams and goals and the only virtue that can rid us such fears is the virtue of courage. If you have dreams of arising from poverty to success and riches, then my friend you must have the unshakable courage to take risks because success favors the risk-takers. If you think that you will just sit there and wait for favorable luck to come your way then you are no different from the fella who spills soup on his chin and tries to lick it.

In conclusion, following and applying these laws of success is the sure way of arising and arriving at success successfully. It is a sure way of transforming your dreams into reality, so if I were you, I would make sure to meditate and contemplate on these laws until I understand them without thinking. Then I would find out how they can be used and there after apply them into my personal lifestyle by turning them into my own, special ***personal positive self-talk confessions***.

ARISING BY THE MATHEMATICS OF LIFE

Well, if you say that you are not artistic by nature to paint or create your own unique picture of life, then maybe you can be *A Mathematician of Life* and add, subtract, divide and multiply your life into success. That is, you can create your own equations of life by adding or multiplying the laws of nature that you know will work in your personal life, or you can simply subtract or divide the ones that you feel are not ideal for the kind of life you desire.

Yet keep it in mind that, unless you choose to discover your own, there is no need to re-invent the wheel by trying to create anything new. The laws are already there, pre-set since the beginning of time and ready to be used by YOU whenever YOU are ready. And since the laws are natural and universal, they can be used at any time by anybody, anywhere, and in any culture in the world. In addition, there is no capital needed to make full use of these laws because they are all free of charge. All that is needed is that you know what you want out of your life, be decisive about what you intend to do or not do about what you want and then take personally initiated action without waiting for the influence or free opinions of other people.

So get up, arise and be your own mathematician of life—Nobody will do the math for you because nobody knows what is deep within the equations of your heart or what has been given to you. Even if so, they are too busy painting the pictures of their own lives or mathematically dealing with the whatchamacallits of their own lives. I wish to stress this point because as people we tend to look beyond our current environment in order to find something that is already under our feet:

Everything has been given to you; life and its mysteries have been given to you to live and solve. Laws, principles and facts about life have been given to assist you. Natural resources, people resources and much more have been given to you and in abundance for that matter. All that you have to do is be the Great Mathematician that you already are and think methodically on how to get what you want from what has already been given you!

The Basic Mathematics Of Success:

(\{External Influence + Internal Influences\}Input + Action Output = Reality)

The following basic steps explain how we consciously and unconsciously create our realities through external influences such as; the environment, people around us, the opinions of people around us, the five senses and more. In detail, these external influences could mean any outside thing that can influence our lives such as; circumstances we find ourselves in; the unpredictable weather; people and their random opinions; traffic congestion; animals; television news and many more. These are things that are outside of ourselves and out of our control; whether we like them or not they have the power to influence us yet they exist separately from us.

With constant exposure to these external influences they eventually produce internal influences that in due time affect our actions. By the internal influences I mean those things that are existing within us like the positive and negative emotions of love, peace joy, fear, hatred, anger, and many more. But the main focus in this chapter on these internal influences are the dominating thoughts in one's mind, the emotional desires and the positive or negative self-talk.

Generally the External and Internal influences that affect our realities can be categorized as follows:

A) *External Influences: 1. Circumstances 2. People 3. Environment 4. The Senses 5. Time*

B) *Internal Influences: 1. Thoughts 2. Emotions 3. Believes 4. Attitudes 5. Desires.*

Anyway, from the brief explanation above, we can deduce the following basic equations step by step to see how we create our reality:

Firstly:

1. External Influence = Internal Influence
(Our External Influences produce Our Internal Influences)
That is, the external things around us have a
significant impact in developing our inner-selves;
our believes, attitudes, habits, character, etc.

Then;

2. Internal Influences = Personal Action
(In turn, our Internal Influences affect the Actions we take.)
Usually we are moved to action not because of the ideas
we have but by strong emotions behind those ideas.

Therefore;

3. External Influence + Internal Influence = Personal Action
*(Thus it is clear that the Actions we take towards
our goals are as a result of the External and
Internal things that have mastery over us.)*

Which Means;

4. External Influence + Internal Influence
+ Definite Action = Reality
*(The complete formulae for creating our Reality
then is this: External Influences produce the Internal
Influences which stimulate us into taking action.)*

Simple Math:

(Self-Talk + Thoughts + Emotions + Action = Reality)

Here now is some simple mathematics to see how certain categorized external or internal influences affect our reality in accordance to the equations we have either consciously or unconsciously formulated. These certain influences usually come in the form of negative or positive self-talk, negative or positive thoughts, negative or positive emotions and negative or positive action. The results of which is either a negative or a positive reality.

Notes:

PST = Positive Self-Talk	NST = Negative Self-Talk
PDT = Positive Dominating Thoughts	NDT = Negative Dominating Thoughts
PED = Positive Emotional Desires	NED = Negative Emotional Desires
PDA = Positive Definite Action	NDA = Negative Definite Action
PVA = Positive Vague Action	NVA = Negative Vague Action
PSCR = Positive Self-Created Results	VSCR = Vague Self-Created Results
	NSCR = Negative Self-Created Results
PEI = Positive External Influence	NEI = Negative External Influence
PII = Positive Internal Influence	NII = Negative Internal Influence

1. PST = PDT
(Positive Self-Talk = Positive Dominating thoughts)

Positive Self-Talk yields Positive Dominating Thoughts, for you cannot have positive thoughts when everything you say to yourself (and to others) is negative. The thoughts that dominate you are usually as a result of the external influences you allow into you, such as, television, your social norms, culture and the words you use on an everyday basis. The most dominant of these influences is the words you use daily especially against yourself. One of the ways in which to guard yourself against any external influence is to simply control what goes in and out of your *six* senses, using tools such as *"The Art of Detachment* and *PST,"* as described earlier in *Arising By Self-Management.*

2. PDT = PED
(Positive Dominating Thoughts = Positive Emotional Desires)

The thoughts that dominate your mind yield the emotions that affect your decisions. Therefore, if you find yourself having negative emotions, simply check the thoughts you are thinking when having those emotions, you might discover that they correspond to the emotions. For that reason, to alter your negative emotions shift your attention to positive thoughts; do so by modifying your mental dialogue. Lifting your chin up and pulling your shoulders back is one practical way to uplift your mood and emotions. You see, generally, when your emotions are down your chin and shoulders will be down also, so always keep your chin and shoulders up no matter how bad you may feel for it may raise the level of your emotions up.

3. PED = PDA
(Positive Emotional Desires = Positive Definite Action)

When your emotions are positive because your thoughts are positive due to your positive external influence or positive self-talk, then you are on the right track to manifesting the desires of your heart. You will not only be propelled into making positive definite actions towards your goal, you will also move the environment and people around you to jump into the flow of your positive energy in order to help you get what you want and get a piece of the pie for themselves.

Now if you believe in a greater power than yourself such as God, this is the stage where your prayers will most certainly be answered because your prayers will be mixed with positivity and the powerful emotion of faith and supported by concrete actions. Take this formula to heart

4. PDA = PSCR
(Positive Definite Action = Positive Self-Created Results)

Now if you add all the above, PST, PDT, PED to PDA you can be sure of a positive reality. Like the christian scriptures say, *"Faith without deeds is dead."* You may have all the hope and good intentions in the world, but if you do not supplement them with some form of action, then your hopes and intentions are as worthy as a diamond in a pit-latrine. In other terms; your thoughts, emotions and desires are pointless without a definite action to back them up. Hope without action is hopeless and action without aspirations is bootless. Therefore the complete formulae for the Mathematics of success is as follows:

5. PST + PDT + PED + PDA = PSCR
(Positive Self-Talk + Positive Dominating Thoughts + Positive Emotional Desires + Positive Definite Action = Positive Self-Created Results)

Positive Self-Talk that yields Positive Dominating Thoughts, which in turn produce Positive Emotional Desires, which also inspire Positive Definite Action bring about Positive Self-Created Results, that is, your Reality. In order to have positive results in your life, you first need to take control of all the external things that may influence your thoughts and emotions because the actions you will take towards creating your own reality are guided by those influences. One of the most effective way to control what goes into your internal influences is through *The Art of Positive Self Talk*, which has been explained in *The Art of Self-Management*.

So far I have been talking about the positive side of things but please keep in mind that all the formulas here can also produce negative results if the external or internal actions are negative and thereby inspire negative action:

NEI + NII + NDA = NSCR
(Negative External Influences that generate Negative Internal Influences, which in turn induce Negative Definite Action, abet Negative Self-Created Results)

That is, a negative external influence such as negative self-talk will produce a negative internal influence such as a negative dominating thought, which in turn will cause you to initiate a negative action resulting in a negative reality. And when you add emotions to the equation, a detailed formula would be:

NST + NDT + NED + NDA = NSCR
(Negative Self-Talk plus Negative Dominating Thoughts plus Negative Emotional Desires plus Negative Definite Action is no doubt equals Negative Self-Created Results)

Now, I like to keep things simple because I discovered that simplicity is the friendliest way to progress, so I have kept these formulas as simple as possible. But if you on the other hand are a keen mathematician and you like to probe deeper into things, then there are ways in which you can take these equations further. For example:

A) PST + PDT + PED + **NDA** = ?
(Positive Self-Talk plus Positive Dominating Thought plus Positive Emotional Desire plus Negative Definite Action = **Negative Self-Created Results?**)

Or:

B) PST + PDT + PED + **PVA** = ?
(Positive Self-Talk plus Positive Dominating Thought plus Positive Emotional Desires plus Positive **Vague** Action equals **Positive Vague Results?** And who wants vague results?)

Now in order to feed your inquisitive and mathematical mind, here are some homework problems to keep yourself busy later:

A) **NST** + PDT + PED + PDA = 1. *Chaos* 2. PSCR 3. NSCR 4.?
B) PEI + **NDT** + NED + PDA = **?**
C) PEI + NDT + NED + **NDA** = **?**

Feel free to alter the components of these formulae in as many ways as you see fit. My purpose is not to think for you nor to give you definite equations and laws in which you must follow indefinitely. It is to help open and inspire your mind into discovering your inner artistic ability to construct your own creations and be your own mathematician who can solve the problems of life with mathematical precision and boldness. For example, if you are enjoying this math and want to do more you can find a friend and create problems for each other like this:

Find X:
A) NEI + NII + NDA = X
B) X + PDT + PDA = PSCR
C) ?

In summarizing our simple mathematics, a concise step by step summary of all the equations could then look like this:

Step 1.
Positive Words Input = Positive Thoughts Output
Negative Words Input = Negative Thoughts Output
Step 2.
Positive Thoughts Input = Positive Emotions Output
Negative Thoughts Input = Negative Emotions Output
Step 3.
Positive Emotions Input = Positive Action Output
Negative Emotions Input = Negative Action Output
Step 4.
Positive Action Input = Positive Reality
Negative Action Input = Negative Reality

Please take note that a constant reality resulting from a repetitious application of the same equation in your life will ultimately become your destiny. In other words, if you continuously let the same circumstances in your life dictate you thoughts, emotions and actions, then ultimately your destiny will be shaped by those circumstances. Be sure to understand this mathematics of success because more often than we realize it, we subconsciously create our reality through the formulas we have adapted or keep adapting in our lives. In other words, be aware and mindful of the formulas that are creating your reality—Are they bringing you success or failure?

Checking The Mathematics of Your Personal life:

If you, like me, have been haunted by the questions: "What is it exactly that causes me to think, feel and act the way I do?" "Why is it that I find myself doing the very things I wish not to do?" Or, "Why does my life keep taking the very turn I always try to veer it away from?" Then think deeply about the mathematical equations of life we have been playing around with here, you may discover that they contain the answers and solutions to your questions.

In point of that fact, the equations can be used to analyze the realities of the past predict your future outcomes. How? By checking which external things influence the thoughts that are currently dominating your mind and what emotions inspire you into action, you can know what kind of results you will possess in your future. The same goes for analyzing the past, you can do so by checking which external and internal influences have been dominating your being in the yesteryear.

Therefore, in order to keep yourself in check, control the results of your actions and change the outcome of your future results, you must resourcefully change the constituents of your equations. For instance, change your NST into PST and or NDT into PDT or your NED into PED and take PDA instead of NVA. Remember; ***A constant reality resulting from a repetitious application of the same equation in your life will ultimately become your destiny!*** You must sometimes change your equations in order to get different results.

The Mathematics of Life:

The art of Mathematics is in solving problems step by step in order to reach the desired conclusion; And so is life, if you are faced with a problem, do not jump to the conclusion before you have understood all the necessary steps that lead to that conclusion. When the problem overwhelms you because it came to you by surprise, *DO NOT PANIC—**PAUSE** BEFORE YOU ACT* so that your mind is clear and open enough to see the cause of the problem. That way you will be able to find the method in which to solve the problem.

Mathematics is a methodical subject and thus it must be treated accordingly; You reach the conclusion to your answer by solving the problem step by step. The problems in our personal life can be solved the same way and life itself can be lived in much the same way; step by step. Solved in this mathematical way, life becomes pleasurable as no problem can ever be too complicated or confusing to handle because simplifying the problem one step at a time makes not only the problem easy but your whole life becomes easier. Confusion comes when we try to understand and do things too quickly and too continuously.

Just like when you first started the subject of mathematics in primary school and were forced to learn and memorize the fundamentals of mathematics such as the addition and multiplication tables as your first step towards learning mathematics. Like so, in life you must force yourself to learn and understand the workings of the universal laws of life and how these fundamental laws of success (refer to *The Art of Success*) can be used to arise yourself from poverty and suffering, to success and happiness. Failure to understand and master these fundamental laws and yet dream of success is like a primary school student whom while still learning his basic additions and subtractions table, tries to solve an algebra problem in college?

Like the Setswana saying goes, "*Thuto ke thebe*"; education is worth more than money, it gives you a foundation in which you can find the solutions to the problems of making that money. It is like a mathematics teacher who teaches you the equations of life and like the equations that make it easier to solve the problems in your life. Yet keep it in mind that this does not refer to scholastic education alone; anything that you may do in life be it sport, art, school or business, all need a fundamental knowledge to learn of its workings in order to arise by it. You see, just like a house without a solid foundation crumbles down, anything in life without a solid base support cannot stand for long.

Though they may be uninteresting, dull and repetitious, we must not ignore our basics no matter what we do. They are what create clarity in the things to come. When it comes to a group of people who take the fundamentals very seriously, the Japanese are the best. Maybe we can learn from them.

You see, Mathematics is a subject that progresses by building onto the fundamentals that were learnt in the steps that came before. The student of mathematics must follow each step of the way up to higher mathematics. There is no way around this. To be able to solve a calculus problem you must know the equations of algebra like your first name. Yet to have mastered algebra, you must have known and memorized the division, multiplication, subtraction and addition tables by heart.

This requires hard work; practicing, repeating and memorizing these concepts one at a time until they are in your blood. Only after learning each step can one move to the next one. Life is exactly the same way. Nothing succeeds like success, each small step of success leads to opportunities for further and greater successes. In a goal of ten steps, each step is a fundamental of the next step and like a ladder, if you remove some of the blocks of steps, you will not be able to reach the higher steps, instead, you will fall down through those necessary missing links.

Because the mathematician cannot move forward onto the next step until he eliminates all of his confusions and mistakes on his current problem, he must fall in love with the idea that patience and *"Practice Makes Perfect!"* In the same way, we too must learn to repeat whatever it is we must learn until we no longer make mistakes and are confused about it. Often because of our fast-paced life, people tend to be impatient and just hurry through to the final stages as quickly as they can without really understanding the beginning stages. This is owing to the fact that in the final stages is where all the talks, prestige and money are. So we only think about attaining those things without paying attention to the important process of first mastering the beginning stages.

When we hurry through the basics in order that our friends or families can shower us with praises of how advanced and educated we are, we only cause ourselves to fall short of the glory of success. You see, the lack of the basics is what will cause us not to arise high into achievement but force us to fall down easily once we are met with problems and adversities of the advanced stages. Does this make sense?

My friend, Best, likes to quote this quote; *"short cuts in life cuts the life short."* Therefore be patient my fellow peers, practice, polish and perfect your basics. Like the Japanese people, let us strongly believe in making complete and constructive use of the basics, taking all the necessary steps and avoiding such shortcuts which end up *"cutting our lives short."* It is only then that we can become great mathematicians of life, solving the most complex calculus problems of life with ease and speed.

Now, can any mathematician get any answer correct if he copied down the question or the equation wrongly? In the same way, can you and I solve our problems effectively if we do not know what exactly caused them in the first place? Can we reach our desired destination if we followed the law of nature or the principles of success incorrectly? Can we get from *Francistown* to *Gaborone* if we do not know the road that takes us there? Can we answer our teachers if we did not hear the questions they asked? Can we achieve our goals when we do not know what it is that we exactly want? Can we solve the problems of suffering if we do not know what suffering is? We must think about these things careful before we are propelled to act in haste.

I am sure now, that you can see clearly that a good mathematician is one who is careful, attentive and judicious to his problems. He makes no careless mistakes and takes nothing for granted by leaving unsolved or misunderstood problems behind. In precisely the same way, we too must be meticulous about our general life; we must know our habits, mistakes, weaknesses and most importantly what causes our downfalls or suffering in life. This is why *The Art of Self-Management* is of undeniable importance because it shows you how to find the root causes of the problems in your life by showing you how to become meticulous, scrupulous and fastidious in your overall lifestyle.

Just to give you a hint, for most of us the root cause of our problems lies in the negative words we input into ourselves (and also to others) and which later is the basis of our dominating thoughts. And like the formulae we have been studying implies; $NST + NDT = NED + NVA = NSCR$. Make sure to learn as much as you can about the art of positive self-talk and do so as mathematically as you can, for in it could be the solutions to your life-long problems.

A shrewd mathematician can solve the problems he does not immediately understand by simply rearranging the problem and breaking it down into words or numbers he understands. For example, he may take this problem; "$2 + 3 = X$" and rearrange it into; "$X = 3 + 2$." By arranging his problem into a way he understand, he is thus mentally freed to solve the problem quickly and easily.

In much the same way, we can solve our convoluted problems by simply **pausing** (notice that I am talking about pausing again) before we muddle our minds trying to solve the problem we do not clearly comprehend. Then, methodically write it down into a piece of paper and look at the problems not only from our own perspective but also from the perspective of the culprit who created them in the first place. Lastly, with a new outlook and a renewed frame of mind, we are unencumbered to unravel its fabricated mysteries step by step. That is, we can now see the problem clearly, understand it completely, and are aware of any other *"smaller-nyana"* problems that may be hidden within or outside the problem which we readily perceive.

Having understood the mysteries of the problem we can accurately decipher the right equation to use when solving it. Therefore always remember that sometimes what we perceive as complicated problem could simply be small and manageable challenge entangled into a superficially big predicament. Therefore to solve it is to merely disentangle that big problem into *"smaller-nyana"* pieces and solve each small challenge on its own before moving to the next one. This can be a great key in solving all problems, do you not think so?

In mathematics, as in life, the most valuable lesson you can take out of class is not the correct answer you wrote but the method or formulae you used to get to that answer. What good are your riches if you do not know how you came upon them and how to accumulate them again or teach somebody else how to they gain them? What good is striving for success which you might achieve in your old age if you do not enjoy the journey you take towards it in your youth? The treasures of success lie within the adversities you overcame before you reached it—Think about this!

You see, people may rob you of the material success you accumulated over the years, but if you know the methods you used to accumulate those things then what took you years of experiences, trials and errors to accumulate, you can easily get again in as little time as a few months or a few weeks. ***How fast you get it back depends on how well you learnt from your past mistakes and mastered your methods of success in obtaining it***. This is an important thought to remember in life. That is why I keep calling it "arising by falling" because the state of being in success itself is not nearly as important as the process of arising in the midst of poverty, adversities and the failures that take you to that success. Think about it deeply. Said in Setswana; *"Kokwana go swa e e tsaeng, e e ko ntle e a iphataphatela." "Go sotlega go ruta botsipa jwa botlhale."*

*There is no mathematician ever too smart to solve all the problems he comes in contact with. From time to time he gets stuck because "**it is a law of success that to achieve it you must first experience its adversities**."* So if the mathematician meets a problem too perplexing to solve and gets stuck, he does not succumb to frustration, laziness and quits. Rather he goes over his false or mistaken answers questionably, then after they still prove to be wrong, he attends to the initial problem question systematically and redoes the method step by step again from the beginning to the end. Hence in life, get rid of the fear of failure and the arrogant attitude that you know it all and can do everything.

Now it is of course good to have the confidence to try your level best at everything but do not get attached to the idea of never wanting to fail. If you do, when the time comes and you do fail, the results will be devastating to your emotions and well-being, ergo making it easy for you to quit and harder for you to try again the next time. On the other hand when you are not attached to neither victory nor failure, it becomes easy to re-try again when you have temporarily been defeated. Detaching yourself from your actions by not expecting anything from them is one way of arising yourself to limitless peace and continuous contentment.

A serious mathematician is a close friend to his teacher, that way he can get help whenever he needs it. What if you are full-on stuck no matter how methodical you get and how many times you go over the problem? Well, the answer is simple; "Swallow your pride and get HELP." What's more, do not forget to say, "Thank you I could not have done it without you," to those who contributed to your success. For who knows, you might get stuck again and if you do not give your teachers and friends their due respect and credit, how can you expect them to help you again when you are in need of them?

Life is the same way; always give gratitude and credit where acknowledgments are due. Also respect everybody you meet because you can never know where your next help may come from. The person you spit on today may become your cook tomorrow. Treat people this way and you will discover that you never run out of helping hands when you are in dire needs.

We have been rigorously analyzing how we can solve the problems in our lives through a mathematical mindset, so in conclusion we can reckon that *the art of the mathematics of life is to systematically and methodically solve our problems one step at a time.* Thus if you find yourself in a complex or perplexing problem in your life, simply think mathematically and ask yourself, *"What would a mathematician think and do in this situation?"*

Moreover, always remember that while you were in school and were given problems to solve, though you got some problems wrong, you always took the time to solve them as best as you could. In the same way, now that life has given you some of its problems to solve, why do you quit or complain and cry over your problems without even trying to solve them? Are you still a breast-feeding baby that everybody has to solve every problem for you? Do you not know that the same scientific mind you used to solve the mathematics problems earlier in your school life is still the same mind you can use to solve the problems in your current life today?

You see there are no excuses for failure in life because all the tools, principles and equations of life have been given to you. You just need to keep it in mind that; *"The reasons for learning mathematics in schools was not merely to entertain your teachers with their red pens but to teach and show YOU **how to play out the mathematics of your own life!"***

THINK ABOUT THIS MATH UNERRINGLY!

ARISING BY THE ART OF FINANCIAL FREEDOM

I am not going to spend time convincing you how important money is because we all know that money is the medium in which we can materialize our ideas, desires, plans and dreams. What I will tell you is just this: *The importance of money is not to have it but to command it to do for you that which needs to be done in order to get what you want.* In other words, money is the means and road to financial freedom. I write about the details of this art of financial freedom in a separate book in the future because the topic is very vast. Here I will briefly describe to you the road map that you need in order to travel successful to your financial freedom. In particular, the six fundamental yet crucial things that will drive you to *The Art of Financial Freedom*:

Firstly, **Financial Education:** To be able to make constructive use of money, you need to be educated about it. Our government offers great opportunities for its people in order to eradicate poverty in the country and make people both socially and financially stable. For example, there are funds, grants and loans for both the old and the young; both the poor and the rich; and for both the educated and uneducated. Furthermore, our government has taken a step further by offering agricultural products, livestock and many other ways in which all its citizens and in every financial level can utilize to arise themselves beyond poverty and dearth to their desired financial freedom.

Financial Education is what separates the wealthy from the impoverished. It is a necessity in today's lifestyle, yet it is not taught in schools and thus many of us are illiterate of these things. All these opportunities offered by the government pass us by because we are illiterate about them, hence we are financially illiterate. As individuals we must do something about this, our families and government cannot do everything for us. Our families provided for us when we were young and vulnerable, the government is providing opportunities for financial success and wealth. Now we must do ourselves a favor and take personal-initiative to find out what it is that we are being offered and then discover how to use it in our lives.

In simple, financial education is not all about how to use money. It is about knowing where to find it, how to accumulate it, how to manage it, how to keep it, how to expand it and how to spend it. Now most people know about the latter best and know very little about where to find and acquire it. That is why a lot of these government programs to help people towards financial freedom are out yet very few people know about them.

Secondly; ***Financial Acquisition:*** To possess money you must know how to legally obtain it, for obtaining it illegally is like setting a snare under your door mat. According to the recent trends of making money, there are four ways to earn it; *Jobs, Business, Real Estate and Internet*:

1. A Job (Just Over Broke): Although about eighty percent of the people in the world acquire their money through working in jobs, statics also show that nobody ever becomes super-rich by having a day job as a major source of income. It is no wonder that eighty percent of the people in the world are not rich, they are just getting by while the remaining twenty percent do not even have to go to work yet they are super-rich. Now I am not putting down jobs here, every job is necessary in its own right for it contributes to the progress of the nation as a whole. I am simply hinting that maybe to be able to fulfill your desires and dreams, you must do more than trust all your future in the security of having a job?

2. Business (The Traditional Way of Becoming Rich): Besides, a having regular job, owning a businesses is the second most common way of acquiring money. The difference between the two is that in a job it is almost impossible to become financial free and if you finally do, it is after many years of monotonous commutes to work. Whereas in a business; with persistent effort and focus, you can easily become a millionaire in as little time as five years and less depending on your type of business.

As a matter of fact, in some Businesses, becoming a Millionaire in a couple of years is not a long shot at all, many people have done it and many are doing it as we speak. It all depends on three things, one; your input as a person, that is your capital, your hard-work, believe and patience. Two; how powerful your product, service or idea is and lastly; how big you promote and market that product, service or idea.

3. Real Estate (The Blooming Business): The world is changing and our country is changing rapidly with it; the population is rapidly increasing and human development is advancing deeper into technology and structural development. It seems there is no way in which people can increase in numbers and advance without technology and construction, so we must learn to accept and use this turn of civilization to our benefit. In other words, as our population continues to increase and the nation advance in technology and structural development, more and more people need homes to stay; places to work; businesses to run, schools to attend; churches to worship at, and hospitals for their health check. All these necessities require one thing in common, *buildings*.

Although this uncontrollable rapid increase in population, technology, and construction can become a problem as it puts too much pressure on the government or a nation to support its overpopulating citizens. *For the astute business man who arises by falling, this problem holds in it a great advantage to become a millionaire and at expeditious growth.* Put in another way, this is a blessing wrapped in problems; an opportunity packed with a difficulty because in those needed buildings is your chance in making money by them for the government cannot build everything by itself.

This is the *Real Estate Business Opportunity* for you my fellow country men and as you can see it is blooming and blooming faster than we can make money through it! Its opportunities are limitless and it is very lucrative. No professional education is need to succeed in it, therefore YOU too can pitch-in on it! Its secret lies in your creativity, ingenuity, resourcefulness and personal-initiative. You see, *unlike cars and clothes that depreciate with time, properties appreciate, therefore, the business itself cannot depreciate which means that your investment in it can only appreciate into millions of Pula.*

4. Internet (The Hottest, Most Lucrative and Yet The Most Dangerous): The internet is the only way I know in which you can have your business product available to every people of the earth twenty fours a day, seven days a week and three hundred and sixty five days a year as long as the clients have internet access. Unlike all other businesses that require tangible products and physical companies or firms, in the internet business, you only need a working computer and an internet network. To add icing to the cake; these days internet access is as common as cellphone networks and owning a computer is as easy as owning a cellphone.

It is the only business in which you can sell your product (such as e-books or many other electronic information) to millions of people in a matter of months and not years. In fact with the right techniques and experience, you can do it in a matter of weeks and not months. And if you are an ambitious expert of its use, you can do it in days and not weeks, believe me! This is why the internet is the only way in which you can become a millionaire in the fasted and easiest manner possible. But do not get me wrong here, I am not saying no effort is required, you do need to put enough energy and focus in the beginning set up stages so that your business can run smoothly.

After you have set up your business in the initial stages, the business will run by itself without requiring hours of daily input like most traditional businesses. All you have to do is to check that your ads are still running or that your website is still visible to the world. It is not surprising or uncommon to wake up in the morning and discover that you made a lot of money while you were sleeping.

What makes the internet business dangerous is the risk of getting swindled into the countless scams and fraud in the internet. That is, there are a lot of dishonest schemes and money hungry people who will deceive you with false advertising and promises that will lure you into investing all your money into the internet schemes and plots. It is especially risky if you are new and you are not sure of what you are doing. So if you want to start an internet business, I do not encourage you to do the research on the internet itself, rather find a physical-person and set a physical-meeting to learn everything before even touching your computer to get on the internet. This is very important.

Be that as it may, the most dangerous part of doing business on the internet is that there is a high chance of getting initiated into the many snares of evil such as pornography, obscenity and many other filthy tricks used by fiends to snatch you into the world of ignorance, immorality, wickedness and all kinds of darkness. Therefore, unless you possess firm self-control, strict self-discipline and a perpetual sense of awareness, I do not recommend this business for you—Yes it is lucrative but it is not for everybody.

In the past I was fortunate enough to make a lot of money through this business, but my biggest problem was that I was unskilled in the art of money-management. So I squandered all the money I made as quickly as I made it and without even saving or at least giving it a chance to grow. This is why YOU must master the skill of managing money if you want success in any field of your life.

Thirdly, **Financial Management:** Money-management is a skill that will not only enable you to retain money but also empower you to accumulate more of it. That way you can be in a perpetual state of arising without falling. The main problem that most of us have in managing our finances is not because we do not know how, rather it is because we do not pay attention to its details and we do not take coins seriously.

For example, for most of us when we receive change in the form of coins, we get lazy and neglect to count it. Or when we see a five *thebe* on the ground, we do not pick it up because we think that it is too small to stop in the middle of our busy life just to pick it up. Worse than that, we are too shy pick it up because we worry that other people will laugh at us for stopping to pick up such a small amount of money. We fear that they will consider us to be very poor, yet we know that a million pula is not a million if but one *thebe* is missing. To get even closer to home, in our shrewd world today, how many times will a store sell you stuff if you are missing that one *thebe*?

We must learn to pay details to our money because a meticulous attitude towards money is essential in the masterful management of it. It is one of the reasons that some men's business keep on running while others' die after having just started. This meticulous attitude is not an inborn thing, it is a skill that anybody can learn and practice everyday until it becomes a habit. For instance, this skill can be developed by doing other simple things like; keeping and filing our receipts orderly; taking the time to balance our check books; comparing prices before buying anything.

Also knowing our net worth (which is calculated by subtracting our liabilities from our assets), so that we do not spend more than you earn. *Strict self-discipline and self-control is the key to controlling our expenditures.* But research these things on your own so that you can become meticulous towards your money and arise yourself to riches. The Indian people can be a good example to learn from.

Fourthly, **Financial Preservation:** With today's unstable economy and the unpredictable turn of events all over the world, it is imperative that you must save and protect your money for the future.You can never know when a rainy day will come, so the wisest thing you can do with your hard-earned money is to save a fraction of it somewhere safe, where you will not touch it unless it is needed.

Saving a fraction of your money depends on what you are saving for and how much you can afford to save, but if you are religious, the religious scriptures seem to point out that saving ten percent of your earnings is the way to go and many other people seem to recommend this as well. But do your own research, there are many books out there that teach you how to save money correctly. Below are a few of the many reasons in which you must save your money:

> A percentage for safe keeping
> A percentage for emergencies
> A percentage for personal pleasures
> A percentage for retirement

A percentage for children's education

A percentage for children's life after completing their studies

A percentage for Tithing (depending on your religious beliefs)

A percentage for charity and goodwill giving

Besides saving money for the future, saving money in itself gives you two vitally important things for the benefit of your overall well-being in the art of life:

First, A guarantee of security: Like I said, unless you are a weatherman, you can never know when a rainy day may come, but if you have saved enough money for such a day, you will always have peace of mind in the midst of fallings and when many other people are worried about the future.

Second, a sense of self-confidence: Have you ever wondered why when people have money in their pockets, they talk and walk boldly and display liveliness in everything they do? Yet when their pockets are empty, they become skittish and walk and talk with their tales between their legs, saying, "Yes Sir!" to everything they hear?

This is because money in the pocket can make one as bold as a brass but a lack of it, as skittish as horse. If all the reasons I mentioned above about saving money for the future are meaningless to you because you are the person of the moment and like the birds you worry only about today, but you lack in self-confidence, then start saving money. And like I said, there are many ways to save money such as in a bank's savings account or digging a whole in the middle of your hut under your bed. But if you are looking for a safe and civilized manner of saving money, then I recommend you do your own research on the following ways:

1. *Investments such as; Trusts, Mutual Funds, Certificates of Deposits, Bonds, Stocks, Shares, etcetera.*
2. *Real Estates Investments*
3. *Livestock and Assets Investments*
4. Find a respected financial adviser and ask him to advise you on this.

Fifthly, **Financial Expansion:** Now that you have educated yourself about money; found profitable ways to acquire it; managed it successfully; and discovered bankable ways to preserve it from unnecessary loses, why not expand it by forcing it to work for you?

This is the part where you become the boss over your money, the part where you can force it to work for you rather than you working countless hours for it. It is the part where you never worry about spending more than you earn because you are now earning more than you can possibly spend on yourself. This is achieved by creating extra sources of income besides your chosen method of its acquisition. For instance:

1) *Fast Growing Investments, such offshore shares, investments and more.*
2) *Real Estate Investments as mentioned above.*
3) *Extra Businesses besides the one you may already own.*
4) *Agricultural Business, such as a part time horticulture or livestock business.*
5) *Network Marketing business, that will create a residual income for you. That is the kind of income where you do not work for money but money works for you all day and all night*

The potential to expand your income is limitless, you just need to be a go-getter and find out what is actually available for you out there. The key is confidence, creativity and personal initiative. Laziness, procrastination and self-doubt are your enemies. You need to act and take risks.

Lastly, **Financial Expenditure:** What good is money if all you do is acquire it, manage it, preserve it and expand, but not spend it? You see, you do all these things for one reason and one reason alone, to spend it. But spending money is not as easy as people think, you must know how, why, when and where to spend it. Carelessness and thoughtlessly expending money is the reason why most people end up spending more money than you earn. Below are a few examples to enlighten your mind in the expenditure of money:

1) Needs; Spend your money on things that appreciates rather than on things that depreciates. For example, it is better to spend money on buying houses that you can sell at a much higher price in the future, than on cars that will sell at half the price them tomorrow.

2) Health; Financial pursuit is good, but just as knowledge is greater than possession, health must come before wealth. For what good is your wealth if you do not have the health to enjoy it? So make sure to spend more of your money on the things that will maintain your health because with good health not only can you make more money, you will have the strength to enjoy it for many years on end. Also, you can have all the money in the world, but without other things that complete your total wellbeing such as good health, healthy relationships, spiritual satisfaction and mental peace, then financial success resorts to nothing more than added stress in your life. So spend money on those things too.

3) Pleasure; Do you ever hear the saying; "Stop and smell the flowers?" Money is the tool to help you do just that because like they say, "All work with no play makes Jack a lazy boy!" Enjoy your money when you have the excess to spend it. You worked for it, therefore you deserve it for it belongs to you. Why be shy and hesitant to spend it the way you want? I mean if you had the ability to make it, do you not have that same ability and experience to make it again? Stinginess is a quality of those who do not have the confidence and ability to re-accumulate the money they possess either.

4. Charity; Remember the principle of success that we studied earlier; "*Share success and it will share its share with you for success shares with those who share it to other people.*" Well that principle could not be much more suitable here; spending money on some good causes where it is needed the most is the highest form of giving that sows the highest reaping seed. *The price for receiving anything in life is to give that which you can afford to give in your current state.* Money comes easily to those who freely give it.

There is a spiritual explanation in this but besides it, genuinely giving in charity to the orphans, the widows, the old, the poor, the oppressed and the forlorn gives you such an incomparable feeling of inner peace and satisfaction that cannot be experienced in any other way. In addition, there are other side-benefits like being given a good name and reputation, which if the sincerity and humility is maintained; many bigger and greater opportunities to increase your finances in the future will be created and availed to you.

Keep in mind that I am not a financial advisor teaching you the details of how to deal with your money here, there is more to financial freedom than what I described to you above. I only give you ideas and introduce you to the art of becoming financially free, so it is up to you take what I have shared with you here further into your life by doing your own fact-finding. And while you are doing your research and pursuing your financial freedom, remember that in Botswana and most of the countries in the world today, one of the major causes of financial poverty, scarcity and difficulties is the plague of drug addiction, especially *alcohol abuse*. Alcohol takes away the necessary discipline that gives us the ability to control ourselves and our finances. It deludes us into financial ignorance and forces us to unmindfully fall by arising.

For example, while we could be getting educated about money and the financial opportunities available for us, we are in contrast drunk with alcohol, thereby we are unable to think and act clearly. Worse, our health and memory gets destroyed. Rather than spend time doing the things that can help us acquire money, we spend that precious time in the nightclubs, taverns, bars and pubs that take away our money. Instead of paying attention and meticulously trying to manage our money, all we can think about is how and when to spend that final coin in our pockets to get one more beer. As opposed to saving out money and making it grow, we spend more money than we earn because we are unable to control that passionate urge to go out and buy more beer.

If we are to be financially free and let alone succeed in any endeavor we may take, we must do something about this crippling affliction of drug abuse. Our current President is really trying hard to rid us of this affliction, but as individual people, we too must take personal-initiative to recognize this affliction as not only a problem that is affecting the nation but most especially our individual lives.

ARISING BY THE ART OF NATURE

Apart from arising by people, arising by God and arising by falling, you can also arise by yourself by learning from the art of nature. In the art of nature, everything we need or want to learn is all around us, we do not need to re-invent the wheel in order that we may save our energy and time for other things we intend to do. Nature holds all the keys to success as long as we have the patience to pay attention to it. Hence, I have included this bonus chapter from the book, *The Art of Life*, so that you can learn how to learn from nature and arise yourself to unlimited heights of success and contentment. Here then is what nature teaches you:

IF YOU WANT SUCCESS BE . . .

. . . As Systematic As a Bee:

They are clean and diligent; they are orderly and build their house in a systematic pattern thus making it easy to do their jobs effectively. They live in the present fully and fruitfully yet still preparing for the future. They are the best at division of labor and specialization for example; there are workings bees that go out to research and working bees that go out to gather food. There are soldiers bees that protect their homes, protect other bees and especially their Queen because they know that the queen is responsible for the continuation of their generation. And all this time they do not compete with each other for their talents because they know that everyone is unique and special in his own way and therefore, there is no need for competition because there is plenty of honey out there and everyone has his own given purpose to fulfill.

. . . As Persistent As a Honey Badger:

If you want to learn the martial attitude of "no retreat no surrender" then look no further than the honey badger. Like its name suggest, if it wants honey, it will get it from the bees by force. No matter how much it can get stung, it will endure the pain until it has obtained its objective, the honey. If it is attacked by other wild animals it fights back aggressively no matter how many enemies it faces. In fact if it is outnumbered it fights patiently until its enemies start getting tired and then takes advantage of the situation. It never gives up. Whatever it grabs, it never lets go until it is satisfied that it has done its job. Have you ever watched the movie *The Gods Must Be Crazy*? If you have not watch it and learn of the honey badger's persistency.

. . . As Tolerating and Forgiving As a Dog:

A dog is one of the most loving animal, yet very few acknowledged and appreciated. No matter how badly you treat it, it will always come back to you when you call for it. If you treat it good, it will show you its love as usual, if you treat it bad it will immediately give you the personal space you desire during that emotional roller coster of yours. However, once you have recovered yourself and want to play with it again it will still run to you lovingly. You see a dog loves unconditionally, but it is not attached to its love so no matter how you may jeopardize your relationship with it, it does not hold it in against you because it is tolerating and gives you room for mistakes. Therefore as a result, it does not live in the past and forgives you easily when you want your friendship with it back.

With this kind of detachment, tolerance and forgiveness, human relations would surely go far if we would learn from the dog. There is a lot to learn as to why the dog is a "man's best friend." It gives you the attention you want when YOU want it. It plays the games you want to play when YOU want to play and thereby makes you feel significant and important. It knows best at the concepts of arising by people as described in the book, Arising By People.

. . . Relentless as a Dung Beetle:

Have you ever watched the dung beetle roll around the dung to turn it into a nice ball three times its size? Around and round it moves to roll the dung, up the slope, down the slope it pushes its dung and turns makes it into a perfect ball. Through the bushes, during the burning sun, in the middle of the freezing weather it continues on and on until its dung becomes a nice little ball. If the wind blows it away from its ball, or the human kicks its ball away, it does not give up, it searches until it finds its ball of dung and rolls around and round until it grows into the size it wants, four times its size. The dung falls into muddy waters, it rolls it. The dung rolls onto all kinds of soil, feces and unidentified objects, it keeps rolling until the ball of dung grows into the size it has envisioned, by now probably three times its size.

Nothing can ever stop the dung beetle from rolling its dung. It is relentless, persistent and tenacious. If you decide to break and scatter its precious dung which it has spent countless hours of hard work working on, well, the dung beetle couldn't care less. No problem; it starts again and rolls its dung until YOU, its other hardships and adversities on the other hand give up and it accomplishes its project—A perfect little ball of dung. Why it spends so much time and energy rolling unwanted animal waste, nobody knows for its business is its own. Like *Chuck Norris*, if you the sadistic snake of its progress decide to bite down its work, well, only you the perpetrator will run home squealing in pain and agony of failure. If I were you, I would not waste my time trying to step on its ball of dung, instead I would try to see what I could learn from it.

. . . As Clever As A Hare:

In African folk stories, the hair is always considered the cleverest animal in the forest. It is not without reason that it is given such a prestigious title. Ask the bush man, the hunters and their dogs and they will tell you. When you chase a hare in the bush, it runs in accordance to your rhythm or pace; when you run it runs, when you stop to listen to it, it stops and listens to you. Before you see it and you talk in your normal voice it will remain in its protected spot and ignore you, but when you suddenly change your voice pattern because you saw it do not want to make noise and scare it, hard luck my friend, it knows it and runs away before you can even creep close. If it so happens that you are now in hot pursuit behind it, it does not run straight, it runs in zig-zag and stops a few meters away to watch you fall on your face in your pathetic attempt to dive and catch it.

If you want to escape from the hot pursuits of failure and poverty in your life, then be as clever as the hare my friend; learn about the tricks of failure and overcome them with cleverly devised tricks of your own. You see, the best solution to solving a problem is in first discovering the root cause of the problem; the best way to defeat your enemy is to know his strategies and plans. So just as the hare knows the tricks of his enemy and the slippery speed he has over his enemy, you too must know your strengths and use them against the strengths that you know the enemy will try to use against you.

. . . As Quick-Witted as a Warthog:

If a warthog is attacked by a gang of dogs or other animals, rather than give its attackers its behind, it backs up against a tree so that nothing comes at it from behind. That way no attack comes unseen. In the same way if you are attacked by people on the streets, back up against a wall and use the wall as your shield; when you do this you have a chance to defend yourself because you can see all your attackers. Besides martial self-defense, in business, you can beat your competitors much easier if you know where they stand in business as compared to you. Do not let them attack you from behind, be vigilant and alert at all times, making sure you are away of every strategy they may use to steal your ideas or clients from you. You see turning a blind eye to your competitors strategies to capture the market is liking giving them your back to stab.

Do not be over-confidence about anything, no matter how good you are there is always somebody better, if there is not, well somebody out there is training and preparing to beat you the minute you drop down your guard. If you think you are training or planning three hours a day to beat your adversaries, remember they are spending six. If you decide you are going to spend three hours of preparations more than them because you discovered that they were spending six hours instead of three like you, well, I am sorry to disappoint you, somebody else is now spending twelve. In life there is never a time to let down your guard, like the warthog you must always keep your front to the enemy no matter what. A perpetual state of awareness is something you must practice everyday and every minute. Buddha had the best way of putting it:

"Mindfulness is the way to deathlessness, unmindfulness is the way to death. Those who are mindful to do not die but those who

are unmindful are as if already dead." The warthog knows this and so should you!

. . . As Decisive as a Lion:

Do you know what makes the lion "the king of the jungle?" It is not that it has sharp teeth and nails, other predators have that! It is not that they are big and heavy, elephants are bigger and heavier. It is not that they are fast and strong, cheetahs are faster and ants can carry more stuff in their proportion to what they carry as compared to lions. Then why are lions revered by so many animals including human beings? The answer is simple; they are decisive. When they make a decision they do not go back on it, they give it a hundred percent focus, determination and effort until they get want they have decided upon. I am not talking about persistence and endurance here, I am talking about the martial attitude of decisiveness. (I talk about this martial attitude in further details in the book, *The Art of Life*.)

It is this virtue of decisiveness that creates powerful leadership, whether in animals or in human beings. A leader who is slow to speak and act but decisive to act is greatly feared by those who follow him. And that is how lions are, they wait patiently before they make their move of attack, studying the rhythm and pattern of the food they are about to catch; watching for the weakest link and the most efficient manner in which to catch it. Silently watching, mindfully listening and patiently waiting and anticipating for the food to make one simple mistake, which would be to stray away from the group or herd, the hungry lion reserves its energy by maintaining its composure. Against its powerful urge to attack caused by excessive hunger, mindfully it waits.

Then, mindful as it is, it has already anticipated the food's mistake. Unmindful, the food "is already dead." In the most decisive attitude ever, it attacks without hesitation. In that decisive moment, there in lies the secret of the king of the jungle; the ability to act decisively and go for the kill. The hundreds of herds that are now scattered in fear do not confuse it, it single-mindedly goes for the one it had already chosen while it watched and waited. And that, my friend, is what we can learn from the king of the jungle; once it has chosen, it has chosen. Once it has decided, it has decided, nothing else matters in that moment. If you have never been on safari, you should go just to see this martial attitude for yourself in action. If you are unable to go on safari, that is ok, simply take out a wildlife video, watch and study how the king of the jungle earns its name.

In combat and sports, this martial attitude of patiently waiting to be decisive is what separates those who win from those who lose; those who live from those who die. If you want to be a revered leader or an admired athlete or fighter, you must learn this virtue from the lion.

. . . *As Family Oriented as a Wild Dog:*

On a more lighter though, you can be decisive but you must still work as a team. Wild dogs can teach us a thing or two about this. They are one of the most collaborative animals; they live in close bonds; unlike other animals and people, they have no territories; they hunt and work together. They do not disdain each other and easily share food by regurgitation. Imagine if families, societies, and nations would live like this? Sharing without selfishness, caring without cruelty, giving without loathing, supporting without jealousy and communicating altruistically, how much would the world advance and in peace? These are qualities that our families can learn for wild dogs.

. . . *As Resourceful as a Human Being:*

I know for sure that amongst the existence of all creatures, human beings are one of the most self-fish and destructive animals, but there is one thing we can learn from them; resourcefulness. You put a human being in the middle of a desert, he will surely find a way to build a house there. You throw him in the middle of cold bush, he will find a way to make fire out of it. You plunge him in the midst of a riverine environment, he will find a way to make boats and travel himself away from it. You cast him on top of a mountain, he will find a way to create his own path of getting down if he wants to. No matter what you do to a human being he will always find a way out. However I am not going to spend too much time revealing the dexterity and astuteness of a human being lest he grows wings. He has the habit of growing arrogant with too much praise.

. . . *As Controlled as an African Elephant:*

An elephant has the strength to break down a tree but still be gentle enough to play with a baby or pick up a needle in the ground. It has the emotional capacity to get into a fierce rage but still maintain control and give you a warning first. However a most significant trait that we can learn from elephants, especially African elephants, is their ability to adapt to any environment, place and time. African elephants can easily adapt to any harsh condition or weather, for example, if you take an african elephant from its warm climate to a cold one, it will easily acclimate to it. I mean look at their size and yet see how they still survive in great numbers today after many harsh years of climatic change, human population growth into their habitats and poaching.

Besides other big land animals that are extinct due to the factors described above, how many smaller animals get exiguous simply because humans are migrating into their natural environment? Many, but elephants do not, they simply habituate themselves to what ever environment they are pushed to. They seem to understand the truth of *The Truth of the Millennium* that; **We cannot always control or avoid what happens to us, but we can always control our reactions to what happened and happens to us!**

Maybe we can learn something from their strength in the self-possession ability which enables them to handle any situation without permanently being moved by it. Also, from the elephants, we can learn that, to be able to handle the big challenges in life, we must have the self-control to deal with the little things. Think about it.

. . . As Independent as a Baby Eagle:

Chris, my friend, had his mother pass away when he was around eight years old, yet I have never seen him beat himself down in self-pity when things do not go his way. Instead his always cheerful, buoyant and full of hope not matter what his apparent troubles may be! So one day I asked him how he does it and he told me; "After about two weeks of taking care of it's newly born baby, the mother eagle takes up its baby and flies high into the sky. Then when it is high enough it lets go of the baby eagle so that it can teach itself how to fly and there after fend for itself. The death of my mother was like that for me!"

Wow! If I was going to feel pity for Chris, I could not have. I mean how do you feel sorry for somebody who does not feel sorry for himself? Chris is still in his early twenties but he is more motivated to succeed than I am. His story is profound and his message powerful beyond words, it is the heart of my message in writing these books, especially my message in the book *Arisings* about *Arising By Falling*. So I am not going to spoil it by attempting to elaborate it for you. You get what you can get from it.

Arising By The Art of Nature was not originally included in this book for it is a chapter in *The Art Of Life,* I only added it here in this book as a bonus for you so that you can learn more about the concept of arising which prevails in all my books. If you want to learn more about arising by nature, then you must wait to read *The Art of Life*. In this book, so far I have talked about *what you must be like* if you want success, in *The Art Of Life* I take it further by talking about *what you must not be like* unless you do not want success. Below is a sample teaser of it:

BUT DON'T BE . . .

. . . *As Shy as a Tortoise:*
Stand up tall lift your chin up no matter who is watching you. Shying away from things will not bring them to you. Success respects those who are bold enough to take risks and face up to their challenges

. . . *As Vulnerable as Sheep:*
Saturate your self with knowledge, train yourself to be competent, practice your speech that you may be confident and eloquent, then that you you will not appear vulnerable to the human vultures that may try to prey on your weaknesses.

. . . *As Crooked as Hyena:*
Do you know that most wild animals, especially predators, will look you directly in the eyes but a hyena is the one animal that will never look at you in the eye? Do you know why? Because it is a crook and a con artist, hence it is afraid of revealing its crooked ways. Well, maybe I am making this part up, but it is true that hyenas never hunt down their own prey unless it is weak and already dying. Instead they are scavengers and will wait for the decisive predators like lions to kill first and then try to steal the food from them or if they cannot (since they are cowards), they stay away a distance and wait until the lions are full before hurrying to scavenge on the left overs. Hyenas are so crooked that they are the only animals that will feed on their preys alive—they

grab and tear away a piece of meat then run away to eat while the poor animal is till alive. After they have finished eating, they will sneak back again and steal another bite. "You don't wanna be like a hyena, I am telling you!"

. . . *As chicken as a Chicken:*

Rather than a hyena, at the least be like a chicken and chicken away from anything that moves. But remember success loves boldness, you can never attain if all you do is run away from everything. A chicken seems not only a coward, it seems to be so stupid it will not even use its wings to fly! How can you be given much and then not make much use of it. We human beings can be like that sometimes, we have all the resources made available to us yet we carp about like chickens when food is practically under our feet. I mean, have noticed how when you scatter food to chicken it runs away from it rather than to it? If you want success, do not chicken away from opportunities when they pass by and you must use whatever has be given to you completely and constructively.

. . . . *As Closed-Minded as a Rock Dassie:*

If any animal can be considered narrow-minded, it would be the *rock dassie*. It does not change its environment and home easily, when running away from danger, it runs back to its home regardless of whether the danger is coming from there or not. Those who know have hunted them, will tell you that before you can chase, find out where it stays, scare it, then run past it and wait for it to run into your hands at its home. The pathetic animal runs so slow that sometimes you would feel sorry for it and play touch with it rather than catch it. My fellow reader, in the hustles of competition, do not be as predictable as the *rock dassie,* change your habits and patterns so that the enemy can never know where you are going or where you are coming from.

. . . *As Careless as Skunk:*

Yes, the skunk has an effective method of protecting itself which is by puffing out an awfully bad odor, but look at its reputation, how many friends does it has? If you are a human being and you protect yourself from people by giving them a bad attitude, not only will you chase those people away from you, that poor attitude creates a bad reputation for you and scares away people around you People who could have become your friends or future clients in business. Bad attitude stinks. Therefore, rather than use a stinking attitude on people, control yourself and do not be susceptible to negative external influences so that whatever people may say or do to you, your remain unperturbed. For remember, ***if you cannot control what happens to you, you can always control your reactions to what happened and what happens***. Unlike the skunk, better learn how to deal with people by understanding the principles in the book, *Arising By People* and you will always have mutually beneficial relationships with all those you come in contact with.

. . . As Inconsiderate as Carnivorous Snail:

In order to strengthen its own shell, the carnivorous snail feeds on other snails by pulling the other snail out of its shell and feeding on it in order to absorb its calcium. As people can we survive for long if we behave like this, stealing each others ideas and riding on top of each others heads without consideration just so that we can get the best view in life? Like a ladder that we use to climb and kick away once we are finished, we treat each other in this manner, oblivious to the fact that in this world we arise by falling with others. Without each other we cannot arise any further than where we currently are. In the future we might need that ladder we kicked away to climb even higher into success. You see, when we arise and take that ladder with us after we get to the top, we can use that ladder to climb higher again.

. . . As Greedy as a Man:

A man? Jealous of himself, he gets so greedy that he creates a gun simply to kill himself because he hates to see himself having more than what he has. He is so selfish that he will do anything in order to get what he wants even if it means destroying nature or other man like himself. Anyhow, I will not talk too much about a man lest he gets angry and shoot me. If you are a man, do not be like the man . . .

INSTEAD, LEARN FROM . . .

. . . The Ant:

Without a leader, they gathers their food in the summer in preparation for the winter. They know the value of work and work hard all day and all night carrying heavy loads of stuff as big as twice their size. All the while they do so without complaint and greedily stealing from others because they know that there is plenty of food for everyone out there.

. . . A Mushroom:

They are the best at arising by falling, sprouting out beautifully from the most unexpected places. For example, while other plants are afraid to grow in an ant hill, afraid to have the roots eaten by termites, they grow there anyway. They are courageous and bold that they could even grow in a middle of a pile of rubbish because they do not let external influences affect their internal make up. Refer back to *The Mathematics of Life* to understand how the mushroom uses the mathematical equations of life as described in that chapter.

. . . A Chameleon:

Unable to change its environment, it changes its self to be at peace with itself and its environment. It is the master of *The Truth of the Millennium*.

. . . The Reptiles:

During the summer, they go out to find food and store it in terms of fat and harvest on it during their hibernation in winter because they know that; "Opportunity likes preparation and preparation needs proper planning!" they know the laws of success. They have understood the principle of detachment and hence easily shed off their old skin when it is worn out and put on new one. In the same way, we too can learn something from them such as not getting attached to the things of the past and thus rid ourselves of heavy old burdens by letting go of the past. Then renew ourselves, make new resolutions and forget about all that tries to weigh us down.

. . . A Cat:

A cat is a good example of the concept of arising by falling; you take a cat upside down, that is its feet facing the sky, and then throw it down to the ground, it will always lend on its feet. In the same way, no matter how life may attempt to throw you down, you can always land on your feet. If you do not, like the cat, simply get up, shake off the dust and move on.

. . . A Human Being:

Yes, there are many things we should not learn from a man, but there are equally a good number of things we can learn from him. With a man, you just have to choose what you can learn and not learn from him. For example; A man can know nothing about anything but use the minds of other men who know about what he does not know in order to get what he wants out of it—I can this virtue "experience without experiencing," and a talk about it in depth in *The Art of Life*. Maybe that is a quality you can learn from man.

. . . *The Trees:*

They lose their leaves in winter in order to avoid loss of too much water through the process of transpiration. By doing so they are protecting their lives so that they can live longer—They too have no attachments. In the same way, as people we can learn to let go of the things that keep us in the past and hinder us to arise so that we can look on to what the future holds for us. You see, no destination can be attained successful if our attention is in the things left behind; to receive more you must open your hands and let go of what you are holding. This can best be achieved by the art of detachment. Learn to be detached like the reptile and the tree.

. . . *The Earth:*

The mother earth accepts a lot of crap—All kinds of crap; animal crap, insect crap, plants crap, people crap, but it never complains. Instead it acquires it all and changes what it needs into beneficial nutrients to produce life. Life that ends up feeding those animals, insects, plants and people. Learn from the earth and you will be able to change any kind of crap that life and people may throw at you to positive arise yourself into the kind of life you desire.

. . . *But Most Importantly Learn from God:*

Just like when you learn about martial arts you can become a martial artist, when you learn about music a musician, teaching a teacher, politics a politician; learn from God and you will become a god yourself. His boundless knowledge will make you boundless in wisdom, his limitless universe cause you to be a limitless being.

This is *Arising By The Art of Nature* for you; learn from it, arise by it but most importantly discover your own.

BOOK CONCLUSION

Since this book was focused on ways in which you can arise by yourself, it is important to make you stay aware that the concept of arising is divided in four parts: *Arising By Falling, Arising By People, Arising By Oneself* (which is this book) and *Arising by God*. Although I have made these parts into four separate book, they are ONE, and therefore should be treated so in order to understand the concept in its totality without partiality. You can also learn about all the concepts in one complete book; *ARISINGS* (a series from the Art of Life). To make it easier for you to understand it all, here is a quick summary from *ARISINGS*:

1) If life beats you down through many adversities, problems and failures; then simply absorb them all and ARISE BY FALLING. For remember, **It is inevitable to meet adversity while on the road to paradise. Success necessitates adversity as a necessary ingredient to its attainment and Life has chosen problems as necessary road to growing and living it!** *To overcome any and everything unfavorable to your well-being; that is, your comfort, health, happiness, then* **the mind MUST arise above and beyond that current problematic situation,** *even if you are presently involved or engaged in it! This is* **the core** *of the art of Arising by Falling, understand it well.*

2) If you want to master the art of ARISING BY PEOPLE and make your dealings with people smooth, pleasant and beneficial, then simply remember the words of a Prophet, **"LET LOVE LEAD,"** *then apply them into you everyday life. Were all individuals,* *corporations, societies and nations to be lead by love like this, then the whole world would be at peace.*

You see, Your sincere **desire to make people feel importan**t *is the* **engine** *that supplies* **power** *to your* **communication skills,** *without it your efforts to communicate will be powerless and your relationships will continue to be no more than a shot in the dark. And LOVE is the vehicle that gives this* **sincerity** *in this desire to make people important.*

3) Now, in ARISING BY ONESELF, always keep in mind that you cannot arise by yourself nor can you arise by others and anything else unless you can first manage yourself.

You see, the key to all management and arisings, depend on your ability to manage and arise yourself at will, for only then can you be in a position to manage your environment, arise by it and arise by others. Most of the times **we cannot control others and our environment, but the one and only thing we can always control and master is ourselves**.

In other words, **we may not be able to control what happens to us, but we can always control our reactions to what happened and what happens to us!** *Knowing this, we can be mathematicians of our own problems and the artist of own destinies.*

4) But, compared to other forms of ARISINGS, ARISING BY GOD is the easiest, fastest and the most gratifying, edifying and illuminating. **For through God we can withstand the adversities life throws at us and bear the weight of the spiritual burdens that unexpectedly come cascading upon our sure-footed realities**. *Through God, the veils of our material world illusions and sensual delusions get removed, our spiritual eyes open and we awake from cosmic sleep and receive Cosmic-Enlightenment.*

5. Moreover, you can also learn that in ARISING BY NATURE, **you can be:**

As systematic as a Bee: As persistent as a Honey Badger: As tolerating and forgiving as a Dog: As relentless as a Dung Beetle: As clever as a hare: As quick-witted as a Warthog: As decisive as a Lion: As family oriented as a Wild Dog: As resourceful as a Human Being: As controlled as an African Elephant and As independent as a Baby Eagle.

However you must not be:
As shy as a Tortoise: As vulnerable as sheep: As crooked as Hyena: As chicken as a Chicken: As closed-minded as a Rock Dassie: As careless as Skunk: As inconsiderate as Carnivorous Snail and As greedy as a Man;

But Instead You Must Learn From:
The Ant: A Mushroom: A Chameleon: The Reptiles: A Cat: A Human Being: The Trees: The Earth but Most Importantly Learn from God:

In conclusion, this was a concise book with techniques and ideas meant to help you arise by yourself in the art of your own life. Its purpose was not to show you definite ways of arising by yourself indefinitely, but to open your mind and eyes to the many ways in which you can help yourself arise from your current unfavorable circumstance or situation to your desired goals or dreams. So do not be limited to the things I have written here, rather discover your own ways of arisings by yourself in accordance to your own lifestyle.

Always Remember that:

Your Down Moments are you best Possibilities for Growth, Your greatest Pains are a way to develop your greatest Resistance, Your worst Failures indeed highlight your Success, Your Loses, your best motivation to Achieve. Your Suffering, your best time for gaining true Wisdom, Your worst Struggles in life indeed are a door way to Greatness, Your closed Doors are but an opportunity to seek fresh Ideas, Your troubles, create your Legacy.

Your Loneliness, your teacher of Self-Reliance,
Your Risks, your opportunities to reinforce personal Initiative,
Your Criticisms, your way to learning more about Yourself,
Your Enemies, your inspiration to act in Love.

Your Fears are the keys that unlock your Courage,
Your Solitude, indeed your time to seek peace and Enlightenment,
Your Hunger, a chance to realize the impermanence of the Body,
And your Death, a time for your soul to experience Freedom! You see, It is by getting burnt that You learn to stop playing with fire.

It is by getting punched in the face that
You learn to protect yourself,
It is by getting things wrong that You
learn the right way to do things,
It is by lowering your body first that you
can lift yourself off the ground.

It is by climbing up the hill that You develop
the strongest forward motion,
It is by taking a step back that You can vividly
see that which is too close to perceive,
It is by pushing the biggest rocks in life that You
develop your strongest will and character.
It is clear then that to advance to higher altitudes
in life WE must first experience the low falls.

The ground is the base in which we can push ourselves
off to the moon, without it no flight is possible!
You See, We Arise By Falling In Our Personal Struggles To Succeed!

Believe and *Be; Wealthy, Healthy* and *Wise.*

AUTHOR'S BIOGRAPHY

Born in Botswana, raised without a sliver spoon by a single mother, Advent AM Monyatsiwa, nevertheless attended private schools where he always displayed an above average academic talent. But his most prominent talent was in his ability to express himself vividly through the works of art, he won numerous art awards in some of the prestigious competitions in his regions and passed his IGCSE exams with a merit, where art was one of the subject in which he got an A* (A star), making him the only student in the country to get an A* in that particular subject.

Art was his natural talent, but he also had other aptitudes in education, athletics and sports; he was always one of the top soccer and rugby player in the school teams and was at one point chosen to play for the Country's under twenty rugby team. Beyond all that, he developed a strong passion for Martial Arts, Philosophy and Motivational Speaking. He was no doubt a gifted individual. But when life strongly gives you something in a certain area, it takes away in another, because, being brought up by a single mother and growing up surrounded by females (his grandmother had six children all females and all brought up without a father), he lacked the one thing he hungered for the most; the wisdom and guidance of a male figure.

Maybe this lack is what made him the man he is today, for it forced him, the little boy, to become a responsible man at a young age. Fortunately for him, his mother (although she too was alone and struggling) always wanted the best for him and the two made an unbeatable team. So due to their team effort, he went on alone to continue his college education in America where he had a series of ups and downs, and adventures that got him acting as a stunt man in low budget movies and also acting a major role in one of the American Television Shows. He was also sponsored by some of the reputable Sports Companies in that country such as Gatorade, for his athletic and Martial Arts talent.

Yet with only one year left to complete his university studies and a life of money and fame in America, he put his education on hold, pushed everything else aside and flew to Japan in pursuit of his dream to participate in the 2012 London Olympic Games. Unfortunately for him, things did not go his way, due to lack of sufficient time, proper preparation and insufficient finances, his dream did not materialize. And by the way, this was not the first time he had attempted to participate in the Olympics Games, in the 2008 Beijing Olympics, he had also failed due to the same reasons; lack of time, resources, finances and moral support. Fate repeated itself.

But rather than accept his adversities as his kismet and crumple down in distress and devastation, Advent was instead inspired and inspirited to gather all the knowledge he accumulated over the many years in his travels around the world; studying the martial arts, learning many religions, learning about people, their cultures and languages—His intention was to discover why when people strive so hard to walk straight in the journey of life, they still keep falling no matter how hard they try? Why the failures, poverty and suffering in his personal life yet he had so much talent and potential?

Although, he initially gathered this knowledge to simply understand himself as a human being and force himself to arise again, it was his mother who once again advised and encouraged him to turn his writings into a book that will not only motivate him but also motivate and inspire the many people in the world going through similar circumstances and life phenomena. She also told him by doing so he will be able to accomplish his dreams simultaneously; which are to encourage and help people and to pursue his olympic dream again.

Advent considers himself a go-giver not a go-getter and describes himself as "**An Artist of Life** by the way of the stars, **An Altruist** by Purpose, but a **Martial Artist** by Choice." He says everything else that he does in life is as a result of those three things. In his 27 years on earth, he has been to over twenty countries worldwide; studied four major world religions comprehensively (two of which he holds a diploma), practiced four martial arts intensely (two of which he holds a black belt) and learns four international languages besides his mother tongue.

Although he frequently travels in and out of the country, he is currently living in Botswana and working on becoming a Self-Made Entrepreneur (He intends to establish several *Advent Wellness Arts Businesses* around the country in order to help people with health and wellness facilities. In the future he plans to build *Advent University of Agriculture* for the sake of adding to the inadequate sports facilities and the country's small agricultural sector which is dependent on foreign support.) Advent still has hopes and plans of continuing his education and pursuing his Olympic dream again; but this time with a renewed energy, focus, inspirited spirit and a new out look on life—All by the grace of God.

He says, "For person to become an independent individual and realize his or her dreams, he or she **must be financially free**—Financial Freedom is the door to all kinds of freedom. But to understand life, you must **become its Artist**; to solve problems and predicaments, **your mind must rise above them**; to deal effectively with people, you must take care of **their need to feel important**. To overcome poverty, failure and suffering, you must **arise by falling within them**; to be content and fully enjoy the fruits of success, you must **always be satisfied in and with what you currently have**. To achieve enlightenment, you must **practice the art of awareness and detachment in everything**. And **meditation in God** is the way to do it all—For God is the ONLY solution to the void and emptiness that torments human hearts."